# The Invasion from Mars

# RESEARCHES IN THE SOCIAL, CULTURAL AND BEHAVIORAL SCIENCES

### EDITED BY
### BENJAMIN NELSON

ADLER, ALFRED: Problems of Neurosis: *A Book of Case Histories*. Edited by P. Mairet, Introduction by H. L. Ansbacher. TB/1145

BINSWANGER, LUDWIG: Being-in-the-World: *Selected Papers*. Translated and with critical Introduction by Jacob Needleman. TB/1365

BURRIDGE, KENELM: *Mambu: *A Melanesian Millennium*.

CANTRIL, HADLEY: The Invasion from Mars: *A Study in the Psychology of Panic*. New Introduction by the author. TB/1282

DAVIS, ALLISON and DOLLARD, JOHN: Children of Bondage: *The Personality Development of Negro Youth in the Urban South*. TB/3049

DURKHEIM, EMILE, et al.: Essays on Sociology and Philosophy: *With Appraisals of Durkheim's Life and Work*. Edited by Kurt H. Wolff. TB/1151

FESTINGER, LEON, RIECKEN, HENRY W. and SCHACHTER, STANLEY: When Prophecy Fails: *A Social and Psychological Study of a Modern Group That Predicted the Destruction of the World*. TB/1132

FINGARETTE, HERBERT: The Self in Transformation: *Psychoanalysis, Philosophy and the Life of the Spirit*. TB/1177

GOULDNER, ALVIN W.: Wildcat Strike: *A Study in Worker-Management Relationships*. TB/1176

GRAÑA, CÉSAR: Modernity and Its Discontents: *French Society and the French Man of Letters in the Nineteenth Century*. TB/1318

HAMMOND, J. L. AND BARBARA: The Rise of Modern Industry. Introduction by Max Hartwell. TB/1417

HAMMOND, J. L. and BARBARA: *The Village Labourer. Introduction by H. J. Habakkuk. *The Skilled Labourer.

HEGEL, G. W. F.: The Phenomenology of Mind. Introduction by George Lichtheim. TB/1303

LANDY, DAVID: Tropical Childhood: *Cultural Transmission and Learning in a Puerto Rican Village*. TB/1235

LEWIN, KURT: Field Theory in Social Science: *Selected Theoretical Papers*, edited by Dorwin Cartwright. TB/1135

LOCKWOOD, DAVID: *The Black-Coated Worker. Introduction by Ralf Dahrendorf

MERTON, ROBERT K.: *Science, Technology and Society in Seventeenth-Century England. New Introduction by the author.

MERTON, ROBERT K.; BROOM, LEONARD; COTTRELL, LEONARD S. JR., editors: Sociology Today: *Problems and Prospects*. Vol. I, TB/1173; Vol. II, TB/1174

MOORE, BARRINGTON JR.: Political Power and Social Theory: *Seven Studies*. TB/1221

MOORE, BARRINGTON JR.: Soviet Politics—The Dilemma of Power: *The Role of Ideas in Social Change*. New Introduction by the author. TB/1222

MOORE, BARRINGTON JR.: Terror and Progress— USSR. TB/1266.

ROSEN, GEORGE: Madness in Society: *Chapters in the Historical Sociology of Mental Illness*. TB/1337

SAINT-SIMON, HENRI DE: Social Organization, the Science of Man, *and Other Writings*, edited by Felix Markham. TB/1152

SCHAAR, JOHN H.: Escape from Authority: *The Perspectives of Erich Fromm*. TB/1155

SHERIF, MUZAFER: The Psychology of Social Norms. TB/3072

SHERIF, MUZAFER: *Group Relations at the Crossroads.

SIMMEL, GEORG, et al.: Essays on Sociology, Philosophy and Aesthetics, edited by Kurt H. Wolff. TB/1234

THOMAS, W. I.: The Unadjusted Girl: *With Cases and Standpoint for Behavior Analysis*. Introduction by Michael Parenti. TB/1319

TIRYAKIAN, EDWARD A., editor: Sociological Theory, Values and Sociocultural Change: *Essays in Honor of Pitirim A. Sorokin*. TB/1316

WARNER, W. LLOYD and ASSOCIATES: Democracy in Jonesville: *A Study in Quality and Inequality*. TB/1129

ZNANIECKI, FLORIAN: The Social Role of the Man of Knowledge. Introduction by Lewis Coser. TB/1372

*In Preparation*

# The Invasion from Mars

### A Study in the Psychology of Panic

### With the complete script of the famous Orson Welles Broadcast

by

## HADLEY CANTRIL

*with the assistance of*
*Hazel Gaudet & Herta Herzog*

HARPER TORCHBOOKS ❧ The Academy Library
Harper & Row, Publishers, New York

## THE INVASION FROM MARS

# Contents

# PREFACE TO TORCHBOOK EDITION

ON HALLOWE'EN night 1938, Orson Welles and his Mercury Theatre on the Air dramatized H. G. Wells' fantasy, *War of the Worlds* so realistically and effectively that at least a million Americans became frightened and thousands were panic-stricken. The study reported in this book was launched immediately after the broadcast and gives an account of people's reactions, indicating what appear to be the major psychological reasons for the mass behavior involved.

Since the publication of *The Invasion from Mars* in 1940, I have often been asked whether I thought such a thing could happen again. The questioners usually imply that we are now somehow too sophisticated to be taken in by anything so fanciful. Unfortunately, I have always had to reply that of course it could happen again today and even on a much more extensive scale.

In this study of the most widespread panic of recent times we are not dealing just with a bit of isolated science fiction pertinent only to one particular time and place. As this little book shows, we are, on the contrary, dealing with an episode of human behavior brought about by a pattern of circumstances providing a matrix for high suggestibility. Such a pattern is by no means absent today, though it would now be fashioned out of new and different ingredients. Since the Hallowe'en "Boo" of 1938 we have seen the development and use of atomic weapons; we know about the existence of Intercontinental Ballistic Missiles

(ICBM) and their immense destructive power. And we hear talk of satellites spinning about our tiny globe carrying atomic warheads that could be quickly guided to any target on earth. Such destructive forces against which there appears to be so little protection can only enhance the possibility of delusions that would be even more plausible than the invasion of Martians—and that would not require the combined talents of H. G. Wells and Orson Welles to set off.

A tiny glimpse of this sort of situation was seen in the blackout caused by the electric power failure in the Northeastern United States in November of 1965, when millions of people were plunged into darkness, many of them stranded in isolated places or in subways and elevators. While no major panic occurred, there is evidence that many of the nearly thirty million people involved endured various fantasies and fears as they wondered, in the first few minutes, whether the power failure wasn't, after all, due to something like an ICBM, and that perhaps total destruction would follow hard on the disappearance of light.

However, some mitigating factors not present in 1938 may help to neutralize burgeoning fears and allay anxieties in panic situations today. Television is one such: it could hardly compete with the scenes created in the imaginations of frightened listeners, nor could it adequately picture all the conditions described in the broadcast. Furthermore, the Orson Welles performance and its aftermath have instilled on the part of all major networks in the United States a deep sense of responsibility in seeing to it that such a situation does not occur again. But there are many parts of the world where such a sense of public responsibility on the part of those in control of communications may not be as great, and there are vast areas where radio communications alone is relied on for news and information and where comparable modernized scares might be perpetrated either by chance or by design.

There has been some public education in dealing with crises—learning where bomb-shelters are and the like. But the confusion and subsequent panic which might be caused by power failures, explosions, fires, eruptions and other natural disasters happening in the wake of atomic attacks are clearly to be kept uppermost in mind and to be prepared for at all times by the responsible authorities.

The panic reported on in this book gave me an opportunity to study a situation which one can only hope will not be repeated in any way, shape, or form. But it is also to be hoped that as many researchers as possible will be trained to follow up quickly and systematically whatever disasters do occur, to study the causes of fear and panic, and to devise ever more certain methods of alleviating the fears caused and of educating people in the actions likely to meet effectively the contingencies in the offing.

HADLEY CANTRIL

*September, 1966*
*Princeton, New Jersey*

# *Preface*

ON the evening of October 30, 1938, thousands of Americans became panic-stricken by a broadcast purported to describe an invasion of Martians which threatened our whole civilization. Probably never before have so many people in all walks of life and in all parts of the country become so suddenly and so intensely disturbed as they did on this night. Yet what justification is there for conducting an elaborate investigation of a panic which was, after all, ephemeral and not sufficiently important to be recorded by historians?

There are essentially two ways to rationalize this study: one is hopefully scientific, the other frankly didactic.

Such rare occurrences are opportunities for the social scientist to study mass behavior. They must be exploited when they come. Although the social scientist unfortunately cannot usually predict such situations and have his tools of investigation ready to analyze the phenomenon while it is still on the wing, he can begin his work before the effects of the crisis are over and memories are blurred. As far as the writer is aware, this is the first panic that has been carefully studied with the research tools now available. A complete description of this panic should, in itself, be of value to anyone interested in social problems.

Furthermore, the attempts to determine the underlying psychological causes for a widespread panic in 1938 should give us insight into the psychology of the common man and, more especially, the psychology of the man of our times. From this point of view the investigation may be regarded as more than a study of panic. For the situation created by the broadcast was one which shows us how the common man reacts in a time of stress and strain. It gives us insights into his intelligence, his anxieties and his needs, which we could never get by tests or strictly experimental studies. The panic situation we have investigated had all the flavor of everyday life and, at the same time, provided a semi-experimental condition for research. Students of social psychology should find here some useful research tools. They will see shortcomings in the methods employed and should be able to profit from mistakes which have been pointed out wherever the writer has detected them.

A more practical justification for such a study concerns the educational implications which an understanding of this panic may have. Although citizens are not confronted every day with potentially panic-producing situations, they do face social or personal crises where their good judgment is taxed to the limit. If they can see why some people reacted unintelligently in this instance, they may be able to build up their resistance to similar occurrences. And if they are ever caught in a really critical situation, the information recorded here may help them make a more satisfactory adjustment. At least it will be discovered how superficial and misleading is the account of one prominent social scientist who said that "as good an explanation as any for the panic is that all the intelligent people were listening to Charlie McCarthy." In spite of the unique conditions giving rise to this particular panic, the writer has attempted to indicate throughout the study the pattern of circumstances which, from a psychological point of view, might make this the prototype of any panic.

Localized panics are frequently reported on shipboard, in congested buildings that have caught fire, or in specific areas suffering some natural catastrophe. More widespread panics are comparatively rare. Nevertheless, panics such as that occurring in the United States on the evening of October 30, 1938, are by no means confined to our own country or our own times.

Panics resulting from financial crises and commercial miscalculations are probably as old as commerce itself. Prior to the eighteenth century such panics were generally due to an undersupply of goods, caused by crop failures, political disturbance, or the like. In the later stages of our expanding economy, an overabundance of goods has led to successive crises and business cycles generally accompanied by widespread fears among the increasing number of publics involved.

The most similar predecessor to the panic resulting from the *War of the Worlds'* broadcast occurred on January 16, 1926, in England during a period of unusual labor strife and shortly before the general strike. On that day the traditionally complacent English listener was startled by a description given by Father Ronald Knox (in the customary news broadcast) of an unruly unemployed mob. The mob was said to have attempted demolition of the Houses of Parliament, its trench mortars had brought Big Ben to the ground, it had hanged the Minister of Traffic to a tramway post. The London broadcast ended with the "destruction" of the British Broadcasting Corporation's station. After the broadcast, the newspapers, police and radio stations were besieged with calls from frantic citizens. However, the panic created by Father Knox's broadcast did not cause either as widespread or as intense a fear as the Orson Welles program.

The fact that this panic was created as a result of a radio broadcast is today no mere circumstance. The importance of radio's rôle in current national and international affairs is too well known to be recounted here. By its very nature radio is the medium par excellence for informing all segments of a population of current happenings, for arousing in them a common sense of fear or joy and for enciting them to similar reactions directed toward a single objective. It is estimated that of the 32,000,000 families in the United States 27,500,000 have radios—a greater proportion than have telephones, automobiles, plumbing, electricity, newspapers or magazines. Radio has inherently the characteristics of contemporaneousness, availability, personal appeal and ubiquity. Hence, when we analyze this panic, we are able to deal with the most modern type of social group —the radio audience—which differs from the congregate group of the moving picture theatre and the consociate group reading the daily paper. The radio audience consists essentially of thousands of small, congregate groups united in time and experiencing a common stimulus—altogether making possible the largest grouping of people ever known.

Because the social phenomenon in question was so complex, several methods were employed to seek out different answers and to compare results obtained by one method with those obtained by another. Such an approach seems advisable in analyzing any problem in social psychology. Otherwise, the investigator has difficulty in demonstrating that his assumption has not been "proved" merely because his method would give him no contradictory evidence. Furthermore, should the investigator reach no positive conclusions, he is unable to tell whether his presuppositions and theories are wrong or whether the fault lies in his method. The use of a pluralistic approach in a study such as this is particularly urgent since the phenomenon under consideration was of so transient a nature. Also, so far as was known, no other extensive investigation was being independently conducted on the problem, thus making it impossible to check one set of data and interpretations against another.

Much of our information was derived from detailed interviews of 135 persons. Over 100 of these persons were selected because they were known to have been upset by the broadcast. The names of the persons who were frightened were obtained almost entirely by the personal inquiry and initiative of the interviewers. The names of persons who were listed in the newspapers as having been frightened failed to produce more than a half-dozen interviews. Many more names were finally obtained than could possibly be interviewed with the limited funds available. Every attempt was made to keep the group fairly representative of the population at large. However, no pretense is made that the group *is* a proper sample of the total population, and the results and interpretations of the complete study do not depend on such a sample since these cases can be studied against the background of two extensive statistical surveys made prior to the intensive personal interviews. Twenty-eight persons who were not frightened but who tuned in late to the broadcast were included in the group interviewed.

The interviews were limited to the New Jersey area for reasons of finance and supervision. All names of respondents used in the text are fictitious and identifying characteristics are disguised, but the true flavor of the case studies is preserved. The interviewing began one week after the broadcast and was completed in about three weeks. The regrettable delay in getting to the respondents was unavoidable for two reasons: funds were not immediately available to begin the study; highly trained interviewers are difficult to obtain, and the danger of delaying the interval between such an experience and an interview is probably less than the danger of obtaining an inadequate or unreliable report from an unskilled interviewer.

Quotations have been freely used to illustrate psychological processes which are implied in the statistical figures. They have also been included at times wherever language failed and meaning could be better conveyed by the impression gained from a quotation.

Since the budget of the Princeton Radio Project was obviously unable to anticipate this particular study, the investigation was made possible by a special grant from the General Education Board. The interviews upon which most of the study is based were made by Mrs. Paul Trilling, Frances Ginevsky, Mrs. Richard Robinson, and Mrs. David Green. The writer is indebted to all of these women for their faithful reporting. Mrs. Green was especially inexhaustible and resourceful in gathering names of frightened persons.

Orson Welles and the Mercury Theatre have cooperated in every way by allowing the writer to examine material related to the broadcast. Howard Koch has kindly permitted us to publish for the first time his brilliant adaptation of the *War of the Worlds*. And Mr. H. G. Wells generously gave his permission for the use of the adaptation.

Dr. Frank Stanton, Director of Research for the Columbia Broadcasting System and Associate Director of the Princeton Radio Project, is to be thanked for his methodological advice and his careful reading and checking of the manuscript. The Columbia Broadcasting System has been kind enough to release the original script of the broadcast and the results of two special surveys commissioned by it and supervised by Dr. Stanton.

Hazel Gaudet, Research Assistant on the Princeton Radio Project, was in charge of the actual administration of the investigation. She not only made most of the tabulations based on the interviews, but many of the ideas reflected in the tabulations and the text were contained in her detailed memoranda to the writer. From first to last she was indispensable in the progress of the research.

Herta Herzog made an independent survey of the panic before this study was undertaken. On the basis of her experience and insight, we were able to prepare the interview schedule used here. She made the initial study of the checks attempted by the listeners and analyzed the case studies reported in Chapter VIII.

The author's greatest indebtedness is to Dr. Paul Lazarsfeld, Director of the Princeton Radio Project. He has not only given the writer innumerable suggestions for analysis and interpretation, but he has, with his rigorous and ingenious methodological help, provided the writer an invaluable intellectual experience. Because of his insistence, the study has been revised many times, each revision bringing out new information hidden in the statistics and the case studies.

The author cannot properly acknowledge throughout the text his debt to Muzafer Sherif. Social psychologists will recognize the general theoretical framework of the study as an elaboration of the systematic outline in Sherif's *Psychology of Social Norms*.

Gordon Allport, Lloyd Free and Daniel Katz have all read the study in some form and given critical advice. Joseph Brandt and Datus Smith of the Princeton University Press have suggested ways of making the presentation more readable and interesting for the non-academician. Jack Peterman has worked indefatigably drawing up tables, while Carolyn Taylor and Rose Kohn have labored with memoranda and manuscript.

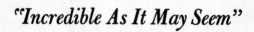

*"Incredible As It May Seem"*

# CHAPTER I ☼ THE BROADCAST

AT EIGHT P.M. eastern standard time on the evening of October 30, 1938, Orson Welles with an innocent little group of actors took his place before the microphone in a New York studio of the Columbia Broadcasting System. He carried with him Howard Koch's freely adapted version of H. G. Wells's imaginative novel, *War of the Worlds*. He also brought to the scene his unusual dramatic talent. With script and talent the actors hoped to entertain their listeners for an hour with an incredible, old-fashioned story appropriate for Hallowe'en.

Much to their surprise the actors learned that the series of news bulletins they had issued describing an invasion from Mars had been believed by thousands of people throughout the country. For a few horrible hours people from Maine to California thought that hideous monsters armed with death rays were destroying all armed resistance sent against them; that there was simply no escape from disaster; that the end of the world was near. Newspapers the following morning spoke of the "tidal wave of terror that swept the nation." It was clear that a panic of national proportions had occurred. The chairman of the Federal Communications Commission called the program "regrettable."

What had these actors said in the brief hour at their disposal? What wild story had they let loose? With the permission of the Mercury Theatre on the Air, the Columbia Broadcasting System, and Mr. H. G. Wells, we are able to print the whole of the radio drama for the first time.

COLUMBIA BROADCASTING SYSTEM
ORSON WELLES AND MERCURY THEATRE
ON THE AIR
SUNDAY, OCTOBER 30, 1938
8:00 to 9:00 p.m.

CUE: (COLUMBIA BROADCASTING SYSTEM)
( . . . 30 seconds . . . )

ANNOUNCER: The Columbia Broadcasting System and its affiliated stations present Orson Welles and the Mercury Theatre on the Air in *War of the Worlds* by H. G. Wells.

### THEME

ANNOUNCER: Ladies and gentlemen: the director of the Mercury Theatre and star of these broadcasts, Orson Welles. . . .

### ORSON WELLES

We know now that in the early years of the twentieth century this world was being watched closely by intelligences greater than man's and yet as mortal as his own. We know now that as human beings busied themselves about their various concerns they were scrutinized and studied, perhaps almost as narrowly as a man with a microscope might scrutinize the transient creatures that swarm and multiply in a drop of water. With infinite complacence people went to and fro over the earth about their little affairs, serene in the assurance of their dominion over this small spinning fragment of solar driftwood which by chance or design man has inherited out of the dark mystery of Time and Space. Yet across an immense ethereal gulf, minds that are to our minds as ours are to the beasts in the jungle, intellects vast, cool and unsympathetic regarded this earth with envious eyes and slowly and surely drew their plans against us. In the thirty-ninth year of the twentieth century came the great disillusionment.

It was near the end of October. Business was better. The war scare was over. More men were back at work. Sales were picking up. On this particular evening, October 30, the Crossley service estimated that thirty-two million people were listening in on radios.

ANNOUNCER CUE:

. . . for the next twenty-four hours not much change in temperature. A slight atmospheric disturbance of undetermined origin is reported over Nova Scotia, causing a low pressure area to move down rather rapidly over the northeastern states, bringing a forecast of rain, accompanied by winds of light gale force. Maximum temperature 66; minimum 48. This weather report comes to you from the Government Weather Bureau.

. . . We now take you to the Meridian Room in the Hotel Park Plaza in downtown New York, where you will be entertained by the music of Ramon Raquello and his orchestra.

(SPANISH THEME SONG . . . FADES)

ANNOUNCER THREE

Good evening, ladies and gentlemen. From the Meridian Room in the Park Plaza in New York City, we bring you the music of Ramon Raquello and his orchestra. With a touch of the Spanish, Ramon Raquello leads off with "La Cumparsita."

(PIECE STARTS PLAYING)

· 5 ·

## ANNOUNCER TWO

Ladies and gentlemen, we interrupt our program of dance music to bring you a special bulletin from the Intercontinental Radio News. At twenty minutes before eight, central time, Professor Farrell of the Mount Jennings Observatory, Chicago, Illinois, reports observing several explosions of incandescent gas, occurring at regular intervals on the planet Mars.

The spectroscope indicates the gas to be hydrogen and moving towards the earth with enormous velocity. Professor Pierson of the observatory at Princeton confirms Farrell's observation, and describes the phenomenon as (QUOTE) like a jet of blue flame shot from a gun. (UNQUOTE.) We now return you to the music of Ramon Raquello, playing for you in the Meridian Room of the Park Plaza Hotel, situated in downtown New York.

(MUSIC PLAYS FOR A FEW MOMENTS UNTIL PIECE ENDS. . . . SOUND OF APPLAUSE)

Now a tune that never loses favor, the ever-popular "Star Dust." Ramon Raquello and his orchestra. . . . (MUSIC)

## ANNOUNCER TWO

Ladies and gentlemen, following on the news given in our bulletin a moment ago, the Government Meteorological Bureau has requested the large observatories of the country to keep an astronomical watch on any further disturbances occurring on the planet Mars. Due to the unusual nature of this occurrence, we have arranged an interview with the noted astronomer, Professor Pierson, who will give us his views on this event. In a few moments we will take you to the Princeton Observatory at Princeton, New Jersey. We return you until then to the music of Ramon Raquello and his orchestra. (MUSIC . . .)

## ANNOUNCER TWO

We are ready now to take you to the Princeton Observatory at Princeton where Carl Phillips, our commentator, will interview Professor Richard Pierson, famous astronomer. We take you now to Princeton, New Jersey.

(ECHO CHAMBER)

## PHILLIPS

Good evening, ladies and gentlemen. This is Carl Phillips, speaking to you from the observatory at Princeton. I am standing in a large semicircular room, pitch black except for an oblong split in the ceiling. Through this opening I can see a sprinkling of stars that cast a kind of frosty glow over the intricate mechanism of the huge telescope. The ticking sound you hear is the vibration of the clockwork. Professor Pierson stands directly above me on a small platform, peering through the giant lens. I ask you to be patient, ladies and gentlemen, during any delay that may arise during our interview. Beside his ceaseless watch of the heavens, Professor Pierson may be interrupted by telephone or other communications. During this period he is in constant touch with the astronomical centers of the world. . . . Professor, may I begin our questions?

## PIERSON

At any time, Mr. Phillips.

## PHILLIPS

Professor, would you please tell our radio audience exactly what you see as you observe the planet Mars through your telescope?

## PIERSON

Nothing unusual at the moment, Mr. Phillips. A red disk swimming in a blue sea. Transverse stripes across the disk. Quite distinct now because Mars happens to be at the point nearest the earth . . . in opposition, as we call it.

## PHILLIPS

In your opinion, what do these transverse stripes signify, Professor Pierson?

## PIERSON

Not canals, I can assure you, Mr. Phillips, although that's the popular conjecture of those who imagine Mars to be inhabited. From a scientific viewpoint the stripes are merely the result of atmospheric conditions peculiar to the planet.

## PHILLIPS

Then you're quite convinced as a scientist that living intelligence as we know it does not exist on Mars?

## PIERSON

I should say the chances against it are a thousand to one.

## PHILLIPS

And yet how do you account for these gas eruptions occurring on the surface of the planet at regular intervals?

PIERSON

Mr. Phillips, I cannot account for it.

PHILLIPS

By the way, Professor, for the benefit of our listeners, how far is Mars from the earth?

PIERSON

Approximately forty million miles.

PHILLIPS

Well, that seems a safe enough distance.

PHILLIPS

Just a moment, ladies and gentlemen, someone has just handed Professor Pierson a message. While he reads it, let me remind you that we are speaking to you from the observatory in Princeton, New Jersey, where we are interviewing the world-famous astronomer, Professor Pierson. . . . One moment, please. Professor Pierson has passed me a message which he has just received. . . . Professor, may I read the message to the listening audience?

PIERSON

Certainly, Mr. Phillips.

PHILLIPS

Ladies and gentlemen, I shall read you a wire addressed to Professor Pierson from Dr. Gray of the National History Museum, New York. "9:15 p.m. eastern standard time. Seismograph registered shock of almost earthquake intensity occurring within a radius of twenty miles of Princeton. Please investigate. Signed, Lloyd Gray, Chief of Astronomical Division." . . . Professor Pierson, could this occurrence possibly have something to do with the disturbances observed on the planet Mars?

PIERSON

Hardly, Mr. Phillips. This is probably a meteorite of unusual size and its arrival at this particular time is merely a coincidence. However, we shall conduct a search, as soon as daylight permits.

PHILLIPS

Thank you, Professor. Ladies and gentlemen, for the past ten minutes we've been speaking to you from the observatory at Princeton, bringing you a special interview with Professor Pierson, noted astronomer. This is Carl Phillips speaking. We now return you to our New York studio.

(FADE IN PIANO PLAYING)

ANNOUNCER TWO

Ladies and gentlemen, here is the latest bulletin from the Intercontinental Radio News. Toronto, Canada: Professor Morse of Macmillan University reports observing a total of three explosions on the planet Mars, between the hours of 7:45 p.m. and 9:20 p.m., eastern standard time. This confirms earlier reports received from American observatories. Now, nearer home, comes a special announcement from Trenton, New Jersey. It is reported that at 8:50 p.m. a huge, flaming object, believed to be a meteorite, fell on a farm in the neighborhood of Grovers Mill, New Jersey, twenty-two miles from Trenton. The flash in the sky was visible within a radius of several hundred miles and the noise of the impact was heard as far north as Elizabeth.

We have dispatched a special mobile unit to the scene, and will have our commentator, Mr. Phillips, give you a word description as soon as he can reach there from Princeton. In the meantime, we take you to the Hotel Martinet in Brooklyn, where Bobby Millette and his orchestra are offering a program of dance music.

(SWING BAND FOR 20 SECONDS . . . THEN CUT)

## ANNOUNCER TWO

We take you now to Grovers Mill, New Jersey.

(CROWD NOISES . . . POLICE SIRENS)

## PHILLIPS

Ladies and gentlemen, this is Carl Phillips again, at the Wilmuth farm, Grovers Mill, New Jersey. Professor Pierson and myself made the eleven miles from Princeton in ten minutes. Well, I . . . I hardly know where to begin, to paint for you a word picture of the strange scene before my eyes, like something out of a modern Arabian Nights. Well, I just got here. I haven't had a chance to look around yet. I guess that's *it*. Yes, I guess that's the . . . *thing*, directly in front of me, half buried in a vast pit. Must have struck with terrific force. The ground is covered with splinters of a tree it must have struck on its way down. What I can see of the . . . object itself doesn't look very much like a meteor, at least not the meteors I've seen. It looks more like a huge cylinder. It has a diameter of . . . what would you say, Professor Pierson?

PIERSON (*off*)

About thirty yards.

PHILLIPS

About thirty yards. . . . The metal on the sheath is
. . . well, I've never seen anything like it. The color is
sort of yellowish-white. Curious spectators now are
pressing close to the object in spite of the efforts of the
police to keep them back. They're getting in front of
my line of vision. Would you mind standing on one
side, please?

POLICEMAN

One side, there, one side.

PHILLIPS

While the policemen are pushing the crowd back,
here's Mr. Wilmuth, owner of the farm here. He may
have some interesting facts to add. . . . Mr. Wilmuth,
would you please tell the radio audience as much as
you remember of this rather unusual visitor that
dropped in your backyard? Step closer, please. Ladies
and gentlemen, this is Mr. Wilmuth.

WILMUTH

I was listenin' to the radio.

PHILLIPS

Closer and louder, please.

WILMUTH

Pardon me!

PHILLIPS

Louder, please, and closer.

### WILMUTH

Yes, sir—while I was listening to the radio and kinda drowsin', that Professor fellow was talkin' about Mars, so I was half dozin' and half . . .

### PHILLIPS

Yes, Mr. Wilmuth. Then what happened?

### WILMUTH

As I was sayin', I was listenin' to the radio kinda halfways . . .

### PHILLIPS

Yes, Mr. Wilmuth, and then you saw something?

### WILMUTH

Not first off. I heard something.

### PHILLIPS

And what did you hear?

### WILMUTH

A hissing sound. Like this: sssssssssss . . . kinda like a fourt' of July rocket.

### PHILLIPS

Then what?

### WILMUTH

Turned my head out the window and would have swore I was to sleep and dreamin'.

### PHILLIPS

Yes?

### WILMUTH

I seen a kinda greenish streak and then zingo! Somethin' smacked the ground. Knocked me clear out of my chair!

### PHILLIPS

Well, were you frightened, Mr. Wilmuth?

### WILMUTH

Well, I—I ain't quite sure. I reckon I—I was kinda riled.

### PHILLIPS

Thank you, Mr. Wilmuth. Thank you.

### WILMUTH

Want me to tell you some more?

### PHILLIPS

No. . . . That's quite all right, that's plenty.

### PHILLIPS

Ladies and gentlemen, you've just heard Mr. Wilmuth, owner of the farm where this thing has fallen. I wish I could convey the atmosphere . . . the background of this . . . fantastic scene. Hundreds of cars are parked in a field in back of us. Police are trying to rope off the roadway leading into the farm. But it's no use. They're breaking right through. Their headlights throw an enormous spot on the pit where the object's half-buried. Some of the more daring souls are venturing near the edge. Their silhouettes stand out against the metal sheen.

(FAINT HUMMING SOUND)

One man wants to touch the thing . . . he's having an argument with a policeman. The policeman wins. . . . Now, ladies and gentlemen, there's something I haven't mentioned in all this excitement, but it's becoming more distinct. Perhaps you've caught it already on your radio. Listen: (LONG PAUSE) . . . Do you hear it? It's a curious humming sound that seems to come from inside the object. I'll move the microphone nearer. Here. (PAUSE) Now we're not more than twenty-five feet away. Can you hear it now? Oh, Professor Pierson!

PIERSON

Yes, Mr. Phillips?

PHILLIPS

Can you tell us the meaning of that scraping noise inside the thing?

PIERSON

Possibly the unequal cooling of its surface.

PHILLIPS

Do you still think it's a meteor, Professor?

PIERSON

I don't know what to think. The metal casing is definitely extra-terrestrial . . . not found on this earth. Friction with the earth's atmosphere usually tears holes in a meteorite. This thing is smooth and, as you can see, of cylindrical shape.

PHILLIPS

Just a minute! Something's happening! Ladies and gentlemen, this is terrific! This end of the thing is beginning to flake off! The top is beginning to rotate like a screw! The thing must be hollow!

### VOICES

She's a movin'!
Look, the darn thing's unscrewing!
Keep back, there! Keep back, I tell you.
Maybe there's men in it trying to escape!
It's red hot, they'll burn to a cinder!
Keep back there! Keep those idiots back!

(SUDDENLY THE CLANKING SOUND OF A HUGE PIECE OF FALLING METAL)

### VOICES

She's off! The top's loose!
Look out there! Stand back!

Ladies and gentlemen, this is the most terrifying thing I have ever witnessed. . . . Wait a minute! Someone's *crawling out of the hollow top*. Some one or . . . something. I can see peering out of that black hole two luminous disks . . . are they eyes? It might be a face. It might be. . . .

(SHOUT OF AWE FROM THE CROWD)

Good heavens, something's wriggling out of the shadow like a grey snake. Now it's another one, and another. They look like tentacles to me. There, I can see the thing's body. It's large as a bear and it glistens like wet leather. But that face. It . . . it's indescribable. I can hardly force myself to keep looking at it. The eyes are black and gleam like a serpent. The mouth is V-shaped with saliva dripping from its rimless lips that seem to quiver and pulsate. The monster or whatever it is can hardly move. It seems weighed down by . . .

possibly gravity or something. The thing's raising up. The crowd falls back. They've seen enough. This is the most extraordinary experience. I can't find words. . . . I'm pulling this microphone with me as I talk. I'll have to stop the description until I've taken a new position. Hold on, will you please, I'll be back in a minute.

(FADE INTO PIANO)

### ANNOUNCER TWO

We are bringing you an eyewitness account of what's happening on the Wilmuth farm, Grovers Mill, New Jersey.

(MORE PIANO)

We now return you to Carl Phillips at Grovers Mill.

### PHILLIPS

Ladies and gentlemen (Am I on?). Ladies and gentlemen, here I am, back of a stone wall that adjoins Mr. Wilmuth's garden. From here I get a sweep of the whole scene. I'll give you every detail as long as I can talk. As long as I can see. More state police have arrived. They're drawing up a cordon in front of the pit, about thirty of them. No need to push the crowd back now. They're willing to keep their distance. The captain is conferring with someone. We can't quite see who. Oh yes, I believe it's Professor Pierson. Yes, it is. Now they've parted. The professor moves around one side, studying the object, while the captain and two policemen advance with something in their hands. I can see it now. It's a white handkerchief tied to a pole . . . a flag of truce. If those creatures know what that means . . . what anything means! . . . *Wait!* Something's happening!

(HISSING SOUND FOLLOWED BY A HUMMING THAT IN-
CREASES IN INTENSITY)

A humped shape is rising out of the pit. I can make
out a small beam of light against a mirror. What's that?
There's a jet of flame springing from that mirror, and
it leaps right at the advancing men. It strikes them
head on! Good Lord, they're turning into flame!

(SCREAMS AND UNEARTHLY SHRIEKS)

Now the whole field's caught fire. (EXPLOSION) The
woods . . . the barns . . . the gas tanks of automobiles . . . it's spreading everywhere. It's coming
this way. About twenty yards to my right. . . .

(CRASH OF MICROPHONE . . . THEN DEAD SILENCE . . .)

ANNOUNCER TWO

Ladies and gentlemen, due to circumstances beyond
our control, we are unable to continue the broadcast
from Grovers Mill. Evidently there's some difficulty
with our field transmission. However, we will return
to that point at the earliest opportunity. In the meantime, we have a late bulletin from San Diego, California. Professor Indellkoffer, speaking at a dinner of the
California Astronomical Society, expressed the opinion
that the explosions on Mars are undoubtedly nothing
more than severe volcanic disturbances on the surface
of the planet. We continue now with our piano inter-
lude.

(PIANO . . . THEN CUT)

Ladies and gentlemen, I have just been handed a
message that came in from Grovers Mill by telephone.
Just a moment. At least forty people, including six State
Troopers lie dead in a field east of the village of Grov-

ers Mill, their bodies burned and distorted beyond all possible recognition. The next voice you hear will be that of Brigadier General Montgomery Smith, commander of the State Militia at Trenton, New Jersey.

### SMITH

I have been requested by the governor of New Jersey to place the counties of Mercer and Middlesex as far west as Princeton, and east to Jamesburg, under martial law. No one will be permitted to enter this area except by special pass issued by state or military authorities. Four companies of State Militia are proceeding from Trenton to Grovers Mill, and will aid in the evacuation of homes within the range of military operations. Thank you.

### ANNOUNCER

You have just been listening to General Montgomery Smith commanding the State Militia at Trenton. In the meantime, further details of the catastrophe at Grovers Mill are coming in. The strange creatures after unleashing their deadly assault, crawled back in their pit and made no attempt to prevent the efforts of the firemen to recover the bodies and extinguish the fire. Combined fire departments of Mercer County are fighting the flames which menace the entire countryside.

We have been unable to establish any contact with our mobile unit at Grovers Mill, but we hope to be able to return you there at the earliest possible moment. In the meantime we take you—uh, just one moment please. (LONG PAUSE)  (WHISPER)

Ladies and gentlemen, I have just been informed that we have finally established communication with an eyewitness of the tragedy. Professor Pierson has been located at a farmhouse near Grovers Mill where he has established an emergency observation post. As a scientist, he will give you his explanation of the calamity. The next voice you hear will be that of Professor Pierson, brought to you by direct wire. Professor Pierson.

### PIERSON

Of the creatures in the rocket cylinder at Grovers Mill, I can give you no authoritative information—either as to their nature, their origin, or their purposes here on earth. Of their destructive instrument I might venture some conjectural explanation. For want of a better term, I shall refer to the mysterious weapon as a heat-ray. It's all too evident that these creatures have scientific knowledge far in advance of our own. It is my guess that in some way they are able to generate an intense heat in a chamber of practically absolute nonconductivity. This intense heat they project in a parallel beam against any object they choose, by means of a polished parabolic mirror of unknown composition, much as the mirror of a lighthouse projects a beam of light. That is my conjecture of the origin of the heat-ray. . . .

### ANNOUNCER TWO

Thank you, Professor Pierson. Ladies and gentlemen, here is a bulletin from Trenton. It is a brief statement informing us that the charred body of Carl Phillips has been identified in a Trenton Hospital. Now here's another bulletin from Washington, D.C.

Office of the director of the National Red Cross reports ten units of Red Cross emergency workers have been assigned to the headquarters of the State Militia stationed outside of Grovers Mill, New Jersey. Here's a bulletin from State Police, Princeton Junction: The fires at Grovers Mill and vicinity now under control. Scouts report all quiet in the pit, and no sign of life appearing from the mouth of the cylinder. . . . And now, ladies and gentlemen, we have a special statement from Mr. Harry McDonald, vice-president in charge of operations.

## McDONALD

We have received a request from the militia at Trenton to place at their disposal our entire broadcasting facilities. In view of the gravity of the situation, and believing that radio has a definite responsibility to serve in the public interest at all times, we are turning over our facilities to the State Militia at Trenton.

## ANNOUNCER

We take you now to the field headquarters of the State Militia near Grovers Mill, New Jersey.

## CAPTAIN

This is Captain Lansing of the Signal Corps, attached to the State Militia now engaged in military operations in the vicinity of Grovers Mill. Situation arising from the reported presence of certain individuals of unidentified nature, is now under complete control.

The cylindrical object which lies in a pit directly below our position is surrounded on all sides by eight battalions of infantry, without heavy fieldpieces, but adequately armed with rifles and machine guns. All cause for alarm, if such cause ever existed, is now entirely unjustified. The things, whatever they are, do not even venture to poke their heads above the pit. I can see their hiding place plainly in the glare of the searchlights here. With all their reported resources, these creatures can scarcely stand up against heavy machine-gun fire. Anyway, it's an interesting outing for the troops. I can make out their khaki uniforms, crossing back and forth in front of the lights. It looks almost like a real war. There appears to be some slight smoke in the woods bordering the Millstone River. Probably fire started by campers. Well, we ought to see some action soon. One of the companies is deploying on the left flank. A quick thrust and it will all be over. Now wait a minute! I see something on top of the cylinder. No, it's nothing but a shadow. Now the troops are on the edge of the Wilmuth farm. Seven thousand armed men closing in on an old metal tube. Wait, that wasn't a shadow! It's something moving . . . solid metal . . . kind of a shield-like affair rising up out of the cylinder. . . . It's going higher and higher. Why, it's standing on legs . . . actually rearing up on a sort of metal framework. Now it's reaching above the trees and the searchlights are on it! Hold on!

### ANNOUNCER TWO

Ladies and gentlemen, I have a grave announcement to make. Incredible as it may seem, both the observations of science and the evidence of our eyes lead to the inescapable assumption that those strange beings who landed in the Jersey farmlands tonight are the vanguard of an invading army from the planet Mars. The battle which took place tonight at Grovers Mill has ended in one of the most startling defeats ever suffered by an army in modern times; seven thousand men armed with rifles and machine guns pitted against a single fighting machine of the invaders from Mars. One hundred and twenty known survivors. The rest strewn over the battle area from Grovers Mill to Plainsboro crushed and trampled to death under the metal feet of the monster, or burned to cinders by its heat-ray. The monster is now in control of the middle section of New Jersey and has effectively cut the state through its center. Communication lines are down from Pennsylvania to the Atlantic Ocean. Railroad tracks are torn and service from New York to Philadelphia discontinued except routing some of the trains through Allentown and Phoenixville. Highways to the north, south, and west are clogged with frantic human traffic. Police and army reserves are unable to control the mad flight. By morning the fugitives will have swelled Philadelphia, Camden and Trenton, it is estimated, to twice their normal population.

At this time martial law prevails throughout New Jersey and eastern Pennsylvania. We take you now to Washington for a special broadcast on the National Emergency . . . the Secretary of the Interior. . . .

### SECRETARY

Citizens of the nation: I shall not try to conceal the gravity of the situation that confronts the country, nor the concern of your government in protecting the lives and property of its people. However, I wish to impress upon you—private citizens and public officials, all of you—the urgent need of calm and resourceful action. Fortunately, this formidable enemy is still confined to a comparatively small area, and we may place our faith in the military forces to keep them there. In the meantime placing our faith in God we must continue the performance of our duties each and everyone of us, so that we may confront this destructive adversary with a nation united, courageous, and consecrated to the preservation of human supremacy on this earth. I thank you.

### ANNOUNCER

You have just heard the Secretary of the Interior speaking from Washington. Bulletins too numerous to read are piling up in the studio here. We are informed that the central portion of New Jersey is blacked out from radio communication due to the effect of the heat-ray upon power lines and electrical equipment. Here is a special bulletin from New York. Cables received from English, French, German scientific bodies offering assistance. Astronomers report continued gas outbursts at regular intervals on planet Mars. Majority voice opinion that enemy will be reinforced by additional rocket machines. Attempts made to locate Professor Pierson of Princeton, who has observed Martians at close range. It is feared he was lost in recent battle. LANGHAM FIELD, VIRGINIA: Scouting planes report three Martian machines visible above tree tops, moving north towards Somerville with population fleeing ahead of them. Heat-ray not in use: although advancing at express-train speed, invaders pick their way carefully. They seem to be making conscious effort to avoid destruction of cities and countryside. However, they stop to uproot power lines, bridges, and railroad tracks. Their apparent objective is to crush resistance, paralyze communication, and disorganize human society.

Here is a bulletin from BASKING RIDGE, NEW JERSEY: Coon hunters have stumbled on a second cylinder similar to the first embedded in the great swamp twenty miles south of Morristown. U.S. Army fieldpieces are proceeding from Newark to blow up second invading unit before cylinder can be opened and the fighting machine rigged. They are taking up position in the—— foothills of Watchung Mountains. Another bulletin from LANGHAM FIELD, VIRGINIA: Scouting planes report enemy machines, now three in number, increasing speed northward kicking over houses and trees in their evident haste to form a conjunction with their allies south of Morristown. Machines also sighted by telephone operator east of Middlesex within ten miles of Plainfield. Here's a bulletin from WINSTON FIELD, LONG ISLAND: Fleet of army bombers carrying heavy explosives flying north in pursuit of enemy. Scouting planes act as guides. They keep speeding enemy in sight. Just a moment please. Ladies and gentlemen, we've run special wires to the artillery line in adjacent villages to give you direct reports in the zone of the advancing enemy. First we take you to the battery of the 22nd Field Artillery, located in the Watchung Mountains.

OFFICER

Range 32 meters.

GUNNER

Thirty-two meters.

OFFICER

Projection, 39 degrees.

GUNNER

Thirty-nine degrees.

OFFICER

Fire! (BOOM OF HEAVY GUN . . . PAUSE)

OBSERVER

One hundred and forty yards to the right, sir.

OFFICER

Shift range . . . 31 meters.

GUNNER

Thirty-one meters.

OFFICER

Projection . . . 37 degrees.

GUNNER

Thirty-seven degrees.

OFFICER

Fire! (BOOM OF HEAVY GUN . . . PAUSE)

OBSERVER

A hit, sir! We got the tripod of one of them. They've
stopped. The others are trying to repair it.

OFFICER

Quick, get the range! Shift 50 30 meters.

GUNNER

Thirty meters.

OFFICER

Projection . . . 27 degrees.

GUNNER

Twenty-seven degrees.

OFFICER

Fire! (BOOM OF HEAVY GUN . . . PAUSE)

OBSERVER

Can't see the shell land, sir. They're letting off a smoke.

OFFICER

What is it?

OBSERVER

A black smoke, sir. Moving this way. Lying close to the ground. It's moving fast.

OFFICER

Put on gas masks. (PAUSE) Get ready to fire. Shift to 24 meters.

GUNNER

Twenty-four meters.

OFFICER

Projection, 24 degrees.

GUNNER

Twenty-four degrees.

OFFICER

Fire! (BOOM)

OBSERVER

Still can't see, sir. The smoke's coming nearer.

OFFICER

Get the range. (COUGHS)

OBSERVER

Twenty-three meters. (COUGHS)

### OFFICER

Twenty-three meters. (COUGHS)

### GUNNER

Twenty-three meters. (COUGHS)

### OBSERVER

Projection 22 degrees. (COUGHING)

### OFFICER

Twenty-two degrees. (FADE IN COUGHING)
(FADING IN . . . SOUND OF AIRPLANE MOTOR)

### COMMANDER

Army bombing plane, V-8-43 off Bayonne, New Jersey, Lieutenant Voght, commanding eight bombers. Reporting to Commander Fairfax, Langham Field. . . . This is Voght, reporting to Commander Fairfax, Langham Field. . . . Enemy tripod machines now in sight. Reinforced by three machines from the Morristown cylinder. Six altogether. One machine partially crippled. Believed hit by shell from army gun in Watchung Mountains. Guns now appear silent. A heavy black fog hanging close to the earth . . . of extreme density, nature unknown. No sign of heat-ray. Enemy now turns east, crossing Passaic River into the Jersey marshes. Another straddles the Pulaski Skyway. Evident objective is New York City. They're pushing down a high tension power station. The machines are close together now, and we're ready to attack. Planes circling, ready to strike. A thousand yards and we'll be over the first—800 yards . . . 600 . . . 400 . . . 200. . . . There they go! The giant arm raised. . . . Green flash! They're spraying us with flame! Two thousand feet. Engines are giving out. No chance to release bombs. Only one thing left . . . drop on them, plane and all. We're diving on the first one. Now the engine's gone! Eight. . . .

### OPERATOR ONE

This is Bayonne, New Jersey, calling Langham Field. . . .

This is Bayonne, New Jersey, calling Langham Field. . . .

Come in, please. . . . Come in, please. . . .

### OPERATOR TWO

This is Langham Field . . . go ahead. . . .

### OPERATOR ONE

Eight army bombers in engagement with enemy tripod machines over Jersey flats. Engines incapacitated by heat-ray. All crashed. One enemy machine destroyed. Enemy now discharging heavy black smoke in direction of—

### OPERATOR THREE

This is Newark, New Jersey. . . .

This is Newark, New Jersey. . . .

Warning! Poisonous black smoke pouring in from Jersey marshes. Reaches South Street. Gas masks useless. Urge population to move into open spaces . . . automobiles use routes 7, 23, 24. . . . Avoid congested areas. Smoke now spreading over Raymond Boulevard. . . .

## OPERATOR FOUR

2X2L . . . calling CQ. . . .
2X2L . . . calling CQ. . . .
2X2L . . . calling 8X3R. . . .
Come in, please. . . .

## OPERATOR FIVE

This is 8X3R . . . coming back at 2X2L.

## OPERATOR FOUR

How's reception? How's reception? K, please. Where are you, 8X3R?
What's the matter? Where are you?
(BELLS RINGING OVER CITY GRADUALLY DIMINISHING)

## ANNOUNCER

I'm speaking from the roof of Broadcasting Building, New York City. The bells you hear are ringing to warn the people to evacuate the city as the Martians approach. Estimated in last two hours three million people have moved out along the roads to the north, Hutchison River Parkway still kept open for motor traffic. Avoid bridges to Long Island . . . hopelessly jammed. All communication with Jersey shore closed ten minutes ago. No more defenses. Our army wiped out . . . artillery, air force, everything wiped out. This may be the last broadcast. We'll stay here to the end. . . . People are holding service below us . . . in the cathedral.

(VOICES SINGING HYMN)

Now I look down the harbor. All manner of boats, overloaded with fleeing population, pulling out from docks.

(SOUND OF BOAT WHISTLES)

Streets are all jammed. Noise in crowds like New Year's Eve in city. Wait a minute. . . . Enemy now in sight above the Palisades. Five great machines. First one is crossing river. I can see it from here, wading the Hudson like a man wading through a brook. . . . A bulletin's handed me. . . . Martian cylinders are falling all over the country. One outside Buffalo, one in Chicago, St. Louis . . . seem to be timed and spaced. . . . Now the first machine reaches the shore. He stands watching, looking over the city. His steel, cowlish head is even with the skyscrapers. He waits for the others. They rise like a line of new towers on the city's west side. . . . Now they're lifting their metal hands. This is the end now. Smoke comes out . . . black smoke, drifting over the city. People in the streets see it now. They're running towards the East River . . . thousands of them, dropping in like rats. Now the smoke's spreading faster. It's reached Times Square. People trying to run away from it, but it's no use. They're falling like flies. Now the smoke's crossing Sixth Avenue . . . Fifth Avenue . . . 100 yards away . . . it's 50 feet. . . .

OPERATOR FOUR

2X2L calling CQ. . . .
2X2L calling CQ. . . .
2X2L calling CQ. . . . New York.
Isn't there anyone on the air?
Isn't there anyone. . . .
2X2L ———

(MIDDLE BREAK)

ANNOUNCER: You are listening to a CBS presentation of Orson Welles and the Mercury Theatre on the Air in an original dramatization of *War of the Worlds* by H. G. Wells. The performance will continue after a brief intermission.

This is the COLUMBIA . . . BROADCASTING SYSTEM (FADE THEME 10 SECONDS) WABC—NEW YORK. (ENTIRE BREAK 20 SECONDS)

ANNOUNCER: *War of the Worlds* by H. G. Wells, starring Orson Welles and the Mercury Theatre on the Air. . . .

(MUSIC)

## PIERSON

As I set down these notes on paper, I'm obsessed by the thought that I may be the last living man on earth. I have been hiding in this empty house near Grovers Mill—a small island of daylight cut off by the black smoke from the rest of the world. All that happened before the arrival of these monstrous creatures in the world now seems part of another life . . . a life that has no continuity with the present, furtive existence of the lonely derelict who pencils these words on the back of some astronomical notes bearing the signature of Richard Pierson. I look down at my blackened hands, my torn shoes, my tattered clothes, and I try to connect them with a professor who lives at Princeton, and who on the night of October 20, glimpsed through his telescope an orange splash of light on a distant planet. My wife, my colleagues, my students, my books, my observatory, my . . . my world . . . where are they? Did they ever exist? Am I Richard Pierson? What day is it? Do days exist without calendars? Does time pass when

there are no human hands left to wind the clocks? . . .
In writing down my daily life I tell myself I shall preserve human history between the dark covers of this
little book that was meant to record the movements of
the stars. . . . But to write I must live, and to live I
must eat. . . . I find mouldy bread in the kitchen, and
an orange not too spoiled to swallow. I keep watch at
the window. From time to time I catch sight of a Martian above the black smoke.

The smoke still holds the house in its black coil. . . .
But at length there is a hissing sound and suddenly I
see a Martian mounted on his machine, spraying the air
with a jet of steam, as if to dissipate the smoke. I watch
in a corner as his huge metal legs nearly brush against
the house. Exhausted by terror, I fall asleep. . . . It's
morning. Sun streams in the window. The black cloud
of gas has lifted, and the scorched meadows to the north
look as though a black snow storm had passed over
them. I venture from the house. I make my way to a
road. No traffic. Here and there a wrecked car, baggage
overturned, a blackened skeleton. I push on north. For
some reason I feel safer trailing these monsters than
running away from them. And I keep a careful watch.
I have seen the Martians feed. Should one of their
machines appear over the top of trees, I am ready to
fling myself flat on the earth. I come to a chestnut tree.
October, chestnuts are ripe. I fill my pockets. I must
keep alive. Two days I wander in a vague northerly
direction through a desolate world. Finally I notice a
living creature . . . a small red squirrel in a beech
tree. I stare at him, and wonder. He stares back at me.
I believe at that moment the animal and I shared the
same emotion . . . the joy of finding another living

being. . . . I push on north. I find dead cows in a brackish field. Beyond, the charred ruins of a dairy. The silo remains standing guard over the waste land like a lighthouse deserted by the sea. Astride the silo perches a weathercock. The arrow points north.

Next day I came to a city vaguely familiar in its contours, yet its buildings strangely dwarfed and levelled off, as if a giant had sliced off its highest towers with a capricious sweep of his hand. I reached the outskirts. I found Newark, undemolished, but humbled by some whim of the advancing Martians. Presently, with an odd feeling of being watched, I caught sight of something crouching in a doorway. I made a step towards it, and it rose up and became a man—a man, armed with a large knife.

STRANGER

Stop. . . . Where did you come from?

PIERSON

I come from . . . many places. A long time ago from Princeton.

STRANGER

Princeton, huh? That's near Grovers Mill!

PIERSON

Yes.

STRANGER

Grovers Mill. . . . (LAUGHS AS AT A GREAT JOKE) . . . . There's no food here. This is my country . . . all this end of town down to the river. There's only food for one. . . . Which way are you going?

#### PIERSON

I don't know. I guess I'm looking for—for people.

#### STRANGER

(NERVOUSLY) What was that? Did you hear something just then?

#### PIERSON

Only a bird (MARVELS). . . . A live bird!

#### STRANGER

You get to know that birds have shadows these days. . . . Say, we're in the open here. Let's crawl into this doorway and talk.

#### PIERSON

Have you seen any Martians?

#### STRANGER

They've gone over to New York. At night the sky is alive with their lights. Just as if people were still living in it. By daylight you can't see them. Five days ago a couple of them carried something big across the flats from the airport. I believe they're learning how to fly.

#### PIERSON

Fly!

#### STRANGER

Yeah, fly.

#### PIERSON

Then it's all over with humanity. Stranger, there's still you and I. Two of us left.

## STRANGER

They got themselves in solid; they wrecked the greatest country in the world. Those green stars, they're probably falling somewhere every night. They've only lost one machine. There isn't anything to do. We're done. We're licked.

## PIERSON

Where were *you*? You're in a uniform.

## STRANGER

What's left of it. I was in the militia—national guard. . . . That's good! Wasn't any war any more than there's war between men and ants.

## PIERSON

And we're eatable ants. I found that out. . . . What will they do to us?

## STRANGER

I've thought it all out. Right now we're caught as we're wanted. The Martian only has to go a few miles to get a crowd on the run. But they won't keep doing that. They'll begin catching us systematic like—keeping the best and storing us in cages and things. They haven't begun on us yet!

## PIERSON

Not begun!

## STRANGER

Not begun. All that's happened so far is because we don't have sense enough to keep quiet . . . bothering them with guns and such stuff and losing our heads and rushing off in crowds. Now instead of our rushing around blind we've got to fix ourselves up according to the way things are now. Cities, nations, civilization, progress. . . .

PIERSON

But if that's so, what is there to live for?

STRANGER

There won't be any more concerts for a million years or so, and no nice little dinners at restaurants. If it's amusement you're after, I guess the game's up.

PIERSON

And what is there left?

STRANGER

Life . . . that's what! I want to live. And so do you! We're not going to be exterminated. And I don't mean to be caught, either, and tamed, and fattened, and bred like an ox.

PIERSON

What are you going to do?

STRANGER

I'm going on . . . right under their feet. I gotta plan. We men as men are finished. We don't know enough. We gotta learn plenty before we've got a chance. And we've got to live and keep free while we learn. I've thought it all out, see.

· 37 ·

### PIERSON

Tell me the rest.

### STRANGER

Well, it isn't all of us that are made for wild beasts, and that's what it's got to be. That's why I watched you. All these little office workers that used to live in these houses—they'd be no good. They haven't any stuff to 'em. They just used to run off to work. I've seen hundreds of 'em, running wild to catch their commuters' train in the morning for fear that they'd get canned if they didn't; running back at night afraid they won't be in time for dinner. Lives insured and a little invested in case of accidents. And on Sundays, worried about the hereafter. The Martians will be a godsend for those guys. Nice roomy cages, good food, careful breeding, no worries. After a week or so chasing about the fields on empty stomachs they'll come and be glad to be caught.

### PIERSON

You've thought it all out, haven't you?

### STRANGER

You bet I have! And that isn't all. These Martians will make pets of some of them, train 'em to do tricks. Who knows? Get sentimental over the pet boy who grew up and had to be killed. And some, maybe, they'll train to hunt us.

### PIERSON

No, that's impossible. No human being. . . .

### STRANGER

Yes they will. There's men who'll do it gladly. If one of them ever comes after *me*. . . .

## PIERSON

In the meantime, you and I and others like us . . .
where are we to live when the Martians own the earth?

## STRANGER

I've got it all figured out. We'll live under ground.
I've been thinking about the sewers. Under New York
are miles and miles of 'em. The main ones are big
enough for anybody. Then there's cellars, vaults, under-
ground storerooms, railway tunnels, subways. You begin to see, eh? And we'll get a bunch of strong men together. No weak ones, that rubbish, out.

## PIERSON

And you meant me to go?

## STRANGER

Well, I gave you a chance didn't I?

## PIERSON

We won't quarrel about that. Go on.

## STRANGER

And we've got to make safe places for us to stay in,
see, and get all the books we can—science books. That's
where men like you come in, see? We'll raid the mu-
seums, we'll even spy on the Martians. It may not be so
much we have to learn before—just imagine this: four
or five of their own fighting machines suddenly start
off—heat-rays right and left and not a Martian in 'em.
Not a Martian in 'em! But *men*—men who have learned
the way how. It may even be in our time. Gee! Imagine

having one of them lovely things with its heat-ray wide and free! We'd turn it on Martians, we'd turn it on men. We'd bring everybody down to their knees.

PIERSON

That's your plan?

STRANGER

You and me and a few more of us we'd own the world.

PIERSON

I see.

STRANGER

Say, what's the matter? Where are you going?

PIERSON

Not to *your* world. . . . Good-bye, Stranger. . . .

PIERSON

After parting with the artilleryman, I came at last to the Holland Tunnel. I entered that silent tube anxious to know the fate of the great city on the other side of the Hudson. Cautiously I came out of the tunnel and made my way up Canal Street.

I reached Fourteenth Street, and there again were black powder and several bodies, and an evil ominous smell from the gratings of the cellars of some of the houses. I wandered up through the thirties and forties; I stood alone on Times Square. I caught sight of a lean dog running down Seventh Avenue with a piece of dark brown meat in his jaws, and a pack of starving mongrels at his heels. He made a wide circle around me, as though he feared I might prove a fresh competitor. I walked up Broadway in the direction of that strange powder—past silent shop windows, displaying their mute wares to empty sidewalks—past the Capitol Theatre, silent, dark—past a shooting gallery, where a row of empty guns faced an arrested line of wooden ducks. Near Columbus Circle I noticed models of 1939 motor cars in the show rooms facing empty streets. From over the top of the General Motors Building, I watched a flock of black birds circling in the sky. I hurried on. Suddenly I caught sight of the hood of a Martian machine, standing somewhere in Central Park, gleaming in the late afternoon sun. An insane idea! I rushed recklessly across Columbus Circle and into the Park. I climbed a small hill above the pond at Sixtieth Street. From there I could see, standing in a silent row along the Mall, nineteen of those great metal Titans, their cowls empty, their steel arms hanging listlessly by their sides. I looked in vain for the monsters that inhabit those machines.

Suddenly, my eyes were attracted to the immense flock of black birds that hovered directly below me. They circled to the ground, and there before my eyes, stark and silent, lay the Martians, with the hungry birds pecking and tearing brown shreds of flesh from their dead bodies. Later when their bodies were examined in laboratories, it was found that they were killed by the putrefactive and disease bacteria against which their systems were unprepared . . . slain after all man's defenses had failed, by the humblest thing that God in His wisdom put upon this earth.

Before the cylinder fell there was a general persuasion that through all the deep of space no life existed beyond the petty surface of our minute sphere. Now we see further. Dim and wonderful is the vision I have conjured up in my mind of life spreading slowly from this little seed-bed of the solar system throughout the inanimate vastness of sidereal space. But that is a remote dream. It may be, that the destruction of the Martians is only a reprieve. To them, and not to us, is the future ordained perhaps.

Strange it now seems to sit in my peaceful study at Princeton writing down this last chapter of the record begun at a deserted farm in Grovers Mill. Strange to see from my window the university spires dim and blue through an April haze. Strange to watch children playing in the streets. Strange to see young people strolling on the green, where the new spring grass heals the last black scars of a bruised earth. Strange to watch the sightseers enter the museum where the dissembled parts of a Martian machine are kept on public view. Strange when I recall the time when I first saw it, bright and clean-cut, hard and silent, under the dawn of that last great day.

(MUSIC)

This is Orson Welles, ladies and gentlemen, out of character to assure you that the *War of the Worlds* has no further significance than as the holiday offering it was intended to be. The Mercury Theatre's own radio version of dressing up in a sheet and jumping out of a bush and saying Boo! Starting now, we couldn't soap all your windows and steal all your garden gates, by tomorrow night . . . so we did the next best thing. We annihilated the world before your very ears, and utterly destroyed the Columbia Broadcasting System. You will be relieved, I hope, to learn that we didn't mean it, and that both institutions are still open for business. So good-bye everybody, and remember, please, for the next day or so, the terrible lesson you learned tonight. That grinning, glowing, globular invader of your living-room is an inhabitant of the pumpkin patch, and if your doorbell rings and nobody's there, that was no Martian . . . it's Hallowe'en.

(MUSIC)

ANNOUNCER: Tonight the Columbia Broadcasting System, and its affiliated stations coast-to-coast, has brought you *War of the Worlds* by H. G. Wells . . . the seventeenth in its weekly series of dramatic broadcasts featuring Orson Welles and the Mercury Theatre on the Air.

THEME

ANNOUNCER: Next week we present a dramatization of three famous short stories. This is the Co-LUMBIA . . . BROADCASTING SYSTEM.

(FADE THEME 20 SECONDS). 9:00 p.m. B-U-L-O-V-A Bulova Watch Time. WABC—NEW YORK.

*Additional announcements.* Altogether during the broadcast four announcements were made to the full network—one at the beginning, one before the station-break, one after the station-break, one at the end. The following announcement was made to the network on the same evening at 10:30, 11:30 and 12:00 midnight: "For those listeners who tuned in to Orson Welles's Mercury Theatre on the Air broadcast from 8:00 to 9:00 p.m. eastern standard time tonight and did not realize that the program was merely a modernized adaptation of H. G. Wells's famous novel *War of the Worlds,* we are repeating the fact which was made clear four times on the program, that, while the names of some American cities were used, as in all novels and dramatizations, the entire story and all of its incidents were fictitious."

In addition, 60 per cent of all stations carrying the program interrupted the broadcast to make local announcements when it became apparent that a misunderstanding was abroad. Other local announcements followed the broadcast. It must be remembered, however, that the most terrifying part of the broadcast came before the station break. Hence listeners who failed to hear the original announcement had ample opportunity to become frightened.

This broadcast with these warnings created the panic. What was it like?

*"It Was Something Terrible"*

## CHAPTER II ✪ THE NATURE AND
## EXTENT OF THE PANIC

LONG before the broadcast had ended, people all
over the United States were praying, crying, fleeing frantically to escape death from the Martians. Some ran to rescue loved ones. Others telephoned
farewells or warnings, hurried to inform neighbors,
sought information from newspapers or radio stations,
summoned ambulances and police cars. At least six million people heard the broadcast. At least a million of
them were frightened or disturbed.[1]

For weeks after the broadcast, newspapers carried
human-interest stories relating the shock and terror of
local citizens. Men and women throughout the country
could have described their feelings and reactions on that
fateful evening. Our own interviewers and correspon-
dents gathered hundreds of accounts. A few of these
selected almost at random will give us a glimpse of the
excitement. Let the people speak for themselves.

"I knew it was something terrible and I was frightened," said Mrs. Ferguson, a northern New Jersey
housewife, to the inquiring interviewer. "But I didn't
know just what it was. I couldn't make myself believe
it was the end of the world. I've always heard that when
the world would come to an end, it would come so fast
nobody would know—so why should God get in touch
with this announcer? When they told us what road to
take and get up over the hills and the children began to
cry, the family decided to go out. We took blankets and
my granddaughter wanted to take the cat and the

[1] See p. 58 below.

canary. We were outside the garage when the neighbor's boy came back and told us it was a play."

From a small midwestern town came Joseph Hendley's report. "That Hallowe'en Boo sure had our family on its knees before the program was half over. God knows but we prayed to Him last Sunday. It was a lesson in more than one thing to us. My mother went out and looked for Mars. Dad was hard to convince or skeptical or sumpin', but he even got to believing it. Brother Joe, as usual, got more excited than he could show. Brother George wasn't home. Aunt Grace, a good Catholic, began to pray with Uncle Henry. Lily got sick to her stomach. I don't know what I did exactly but I know I prayed harder and more earnestly than ever before. Just as soon as we were convinced that this thing was real, how pretty all things on earth seemed; how soon we put our trust in God."

Archie Burbank, a filling station operator in Newark, described his reactions. "My girl friend and I stayed in the car for awhile, just driving around. Then we followed the lead of a friend. All of us ran into a grocery store and asked the man if we could go into his cellar. He said, 'What's the matter? Are you trying to ruin my business?' So he chased us out. A crowd collected. We rushed to an apartment house and asked the man in the apartment to let us in his cellar. He said, 'I don't have any cellar! Get away!' Then people started to rush out of the apartment house all undressed. We got into the car and listened some more. Suddenly, the announcer was gassed, the station went dead so we tried another station but nothing would come on. Then we went to a gas station and filled up our tank in preparation for just riding as far as we could. The gas station man didn't know anything about it. Then one friend, male, decided he would call up the *Newark Evening News*. He found out it was a play. We listened to the rest of the play and then went dancing."

Mrs. Joslin, who lives in a poor section of a large eastern city and whose husband is a day laborer, said, "I was terribly frightened. I wanted to pack and take my child in my arms, gather up my friends and get in the car and just go north as far as we could. But what I did was just set by one window, prayin', listenin', and scared stiff and my husband by the other snifflin' and lookin' out to see if people were runnin'. Then when the announcer said 'evacuate the city,' I ran and called my boarder and started with my child to rush down the stairs, not waitin' to ketch my hat or anything. When I got to the foot of the stairs I just couldn't get out, I don't know why. Meantime my husband he tried other stations and found them still runnin'. He couldn't smell any gas or see people runnin', so he called me back and told me it was just a play. So I set down, still ready to go at any minute till I heard Orson Welles say, 'Folks, I hope we ain't alarmed you. This is just a play!' Then, I just set!"

Mrs. Delaney, an ardent Catholic living in a New York suburb, could not pull herself from her radio. "I never hugged my radio so closely as I did last night. I held a crucifix in my hand and prayed while looking out of my open window for falling meteors. I also wanted to get a faint whiff of the gas so that I would know when to close my window and hermetically seal my room with waterproof cement or anything else I could get hold of. My plan was to stay in the room and hope that I would not suffocate before the gas blew away. When the monsters were wading across the Hudson River and coming into New York, I wanted to run up on my roof to see what they looked like, but I could not leave my radio while it was telling me of their whereabouts."

Helen Anthony, a young high school girl in Pennsylvania, wrote that she "kept on saying, 'Where are we going to go? What can we do? What difference does it make whether we get killed now or later?' I was really hysterical. My two girl friends and I were crying and holding each other and everything seemed so unimportant in face of death. We felt it was terrible we should die so young. I'm always nervous anyway and I guess I was getting everybody even more scared. The boy from downstairs threatened to knock me out if I didn't stop acting so hysterical. We tried another small station which had some program on that confirmed our fears. I was sure the end of the world was coming."

Mothers all over the country hastened to protect helpless infants and children. From New England was sent the description of Mrs. Walters. "I kept shivering and shaking. I pulled out suitcases and put them back, started to pack, but didn't know what to take. I kept piling clothes on my baby, took all her clothes out and wrapped her up. Everybody went out of the house except the neighbor upstairs. I ran up and banged on his door. He wrapped two of his children in blankets and I carried the other, and my husband carried my child. We rushed out. I don't know why but I wanted to take some bread, for I thought that if everything is burning, you can't eat money, but you can eat bread."

A mother living in a small eastern town said that "right after we tuned in I had gone out to see my baby, when my husband called to me. I ran in and got frightened right away. I ran downstairs to the telephone and called my mother. She hadn't been listening. Then I took the little baby and my husband wrapped our seven-year-old child and we rode with friends who live on the street to the tavern where my mother works. By the time we got there my mother had the radio on and all of the people in the tavern were excited. I just sat down and cuddled my baby and shook so that I couldn't talk. I was sick in bed for three days after the broadcast."

A mother in a crowded New Jersey tenement "thought it was all up with us. I grabbed my boy and just sat and cried, and then I couldn't stand it any more when they said they were coming this way, so I turned the radio off and ran out into the hall. The woman next door was out there crying too. Then a man ran up the stairs and when he saw us he laughed at us and said downstairs the people were fooled too, and that it was only a joke. We didn't believe him and told him to pray, but he finally convinced us. He said he had called the police, and they told him it was a play. So I went back into the apartment, and just kept crying till my husband came home, because I was still upset."

A senior in a large eastern college returning from a date with his girl heard the broadcast in his car and, heroically enough, decided to return and rescue her. "One of the first things I did was to try to phone my girl in Poughkeepsie, but the lines were all busy, so that just confirmed my impression that the thing was true. We started driving back to Poughkeepsie. We had heard that Princeton was wiped out and gas was spreading over New Jersey and fire, so I figured there wasn't anything to do—we figured our friends and families were all dead. I made the 45 miles in 35 minutes and didn't even realize it. I drove right through Newburgh and never even knew I went through it. I don't know why we weren't killed. My roommate was crying and praying. He was even more excited than I was—or more noisy about it anyway; I guess I took it out in pushing the accelerator to the floor. I imagine having to concentrate on the driving held me together somewhat. On Monday after it was all over, and I started to think of that ride, I was more jittery than when it was happening. The speed was never under 70. I thought I was racing against time. The gas was supposed to be spreading up north. I didn't have any idea exactly what I was fleeing from, and that made me all the more afraid. All I could think of was being burned alive or being gassed. And yet I didn't care somehow whether I hit anything with the car or not. I remember thinking distinctly how easy it would be to get shot cleanly in a war. I remember also thinking there wasn't any God. My roommate was really praying and crying all the time. I thought the whole human race was going to be wiped out—that seemed more important than the fact that we were going to die. It seemed awful that everything that had been worked on for years was going to be lost forever. They kept giving these flashbacks and they made it seem so real. I do remember, though, when the commentator said, 'Pierson and I will go over and report,' and then they were on in what seemed about four minutes, and that seemed too short a time, but we didn't take it too seriously. The mention of towns along the highways with names that we knew, and the names of hospitals we knew, seemed so real."

Two thousand miles away, in a small college of a southwestern state, other college students were equally terrified. "The girls in the sorority houses and dormitories huddled around their radios trembling and weeping in each other's arms. They separated themselves from their friends only to take their turn at the telephones to make long distance calls to their parents, saying goodbye for what they thought might be the last time. This horror was shared by older and more experienced people—instructors and supervisors in the university. Terror-stricken girls, hoping to escape from the Mars invaders, rushed to the basement of the dormitory. A fraternity boy, frantic with fear, threw off dormitory regulations when he sought out his girl friend and started for home. Another boy rushed into the street to warn the town of the invasion."

Sylvia Holmes, a panic-stricken Negro housewife who lived in Newark, thinking the end of the world was near, in her excitement overstepped the bounds of her usual frugality. "We listened getting more and more excited. We all felt the world was coming to an end. Then we heard 'Get gas masks!' That was the part that got me. I thought I was going crazy. It's a wonder my heart didn't fail me because I'm nervous anyway. I felt if the gas was on, I wanted to be together with my husband and nephew so we could all die together. So I ran out of the house. I guess I didn't know what I was doing. I stood on the corner waiting for a bus and I thought every car that came along was a bus and I ran out to get it. People saw how excited I was and tried to quiet me, but I kept saying over and over again to everybody I met: 'Don't you know New Jersey is destroyed by the Germans—it's on the radio.' I was all excited and I knew that Hitler didn't appreciate President Roosevelt's telegram a couple of weeks ago. While the U.S. thought everything was settled, they came down unexpected. The Germans are so wise they were in something like a balloon and when the balloon landed —that's when they announced the explosion—the Germans landed. When I got home my husband wasn't there so I rushed in next door and warned the neighbors that the world was coming to an end. My aunt was there and she tried to quiet me and said, 'If God is coming that way, we just have to wait—go home and be quiet— don't be excited.' I went home. My knees were shaking so, I could hardly walk up the stairs. I found my nephew had come home and gone to bed. I woke him up. I looked in the ice-box and saw some chicken left from Sunday dinner that I was saving for Monday night dinner. I said to my nephew, 'We may as well eat this chicken—we won't be here in the morning.' Then my husband came in. When I told him about it, he wasn't as excited as I was, but he thought it was the end of the world coming, too. He turned on our radio to WOR. It was eleven o'clock and we heard it announced that it was only a play. It sure felt good—just like a burden was lifted off me."

George Bates, an unskilled laborer in Massachusetts spent his savings trying to escape. Somehow he heard of this investigation and wrote: "I thought the best thing to do was go away, so I took $3.25 out of my savings and bought a ticket. After I had gone 60 miles I heard it was a play. Now I don't have any money left for the shoes I was saving up for. Would you please have someone send me a pair of black shoes, size 9-B."

Sarah Jacob of Illinois, a regular listener to the Mercury Theatre, said, "They should have announced that it was a play. We listened to the whole thing and they never did. I was very much afraid. When it was over we ran to the doctor's to see if he could help us get away. Everybody was out in the street and somebody told my husband it was just a play. We always listen to Orson Welles but we didn't imagine this was it. If we hadn't found out it was a play almost as soon as it was over, I don't know what we'd have done."

## Who Listened?

The best direct evidence upon which to base an estimate of the number of people who listened to this broadcast is obtained from a poll made by the American Institute of Public Opinion (AIPO) about six weeks after the broadcast.[2] In a nation-wide sample of several thousand adults, 12 per cent answered "Yes" to the question "Did you listen to the Orson Welles broadcast of the invasion from Mars?" The representativeness of the sample used by the Gallup survey is based on the characteristics of the "voting public." It therefore contains more men, fewer young people, and, probably fewer southern Negroes than the actual radio-listening public.[3] According to the 1930 census there are 75,000,000 persons of voting age in the country.

[2] This delay was unavoidable due to the fact that sufficient funds were available for the survey only after this time had elapsed. The writer is indebted to Mr. Lawrence Benson and Mr. Edward Benson of the American Institute of Public Opinion for their cooperation during this survey; also to Dr. George Gallup for permitting the facilities of the Institute to be used for this study.

[3] For a discussion of public opinion polls and the techniques of measurement, see D. Katz and H. Cantril, "Public Opinion Polls," *Sociometry*, 1937, Vol. I, pp. 155-179.

Twelve per cent of this number would indicate that about 9,000,000 adults heard the broadcast. If we consider all persons over ten years of age, then, according to the 1930 census we shall have 12 per cent of 99,000,-000 people, or, almost 12,000,000. It is undoubtedly true that many children even under ten years of age listen to the radio after eight o'clock on Sunday evening, especially when we remember that for more than half of the country this broadcast was at least an hour earlier than eight p.m. In addition to these young listeners, a large number of youngsters must have been wakened by frightened parents preparing to flee for their lives.

The AIPO figure is over 100 per cent higher than any other known measure of this audience. However, since the Institute reaches many small communities and non-telephone homes not regularly sampled by radio research organizations, its result is probably the most accurate.[4] C. E. Hooper, Inc., a commercial research organization making continuous checks on program popularity, indicates a listening audience of about 4,000,000 to the Mercury Theatre broadcast on October 30, 1938.[5] If we pool the AIPO and Hooper results, a final estimate of 6,000,000 listeners is conservative. Had the program enjoyed greater popularity, the panic might have been more widespread.

[4] A critical discussion of methods of measuring the listening audience, by Frank Stanton, *Measuring the Listening Audience,* is scheduled to be published by Princeton University Press, 1940.

[5] The Cooperative Analysis of Broadcasting report (CAB) did not survey Oct. 30. The Oct. 23 figure is 4 per cent of radio homes; the Nov. 6 figure 7.4 per cent of radio homes. It is not without significance that the program's popularity increased almost 100 per cent in these two weeks and it seems probable that almost this entire jump was due to the excitement and publicity aroused by the Oct. 30 broadcast.

The *regional differences* of the audience are significant. A breakdown of the AIPO figures gives the following percentages of persons who listened.

| | |
|---|---|
| Mountain and Pacific | 20 per cent |
| Middle Atlantic | 15 |
| West North Central | 12 |
| East North Central | 11 |
| South | 8 |
| New England | 8 |

The high percentage of Mountain and Pacific states is undoubtedly due to the fact that listening in general is highest in the far western part of the country.[6] The low figure for the New England states is due to the fact that Columbia's Boston outlet (WEEI) did not carry the program.

Tabulation by *economic status* indicates that the very poor people did not listen to this dramatic program as much as other economic groups: 13 per cent of the people in the upper and middle income brackets and 9 per cent in the low income group had tuned in. The AIPO figures indicate significant differences according to *age levels*: 14 per cent of young people under thirty, 12 per cent of those between thirty and fifty, and only 10 per cent of those over fifty years of age heard the broadcast. No important sex differences in the composition of the audience appear in the AIPO data. Twelve per cent of the men heard the program, 11 per cent of the women.

### How Many Were Frightened?

In answer to the AIPO question, "At the time you were listening, did you think this broadcast was a play

[6] Stanton, *op. cit.*

or a real news report?" 28 per cent indicated that they believed the broadcast was a news bulletin. Seventy per cent of those who thought they were listening to a news report were frightened or disturbed. This would mean that about 1,700,000 heard the broadcast as a news bulletin and that about 1,200,000 were excited by it.

In spite of the attempt to word the question concerning the individual's reaction in a casual way, it must be remembered that the number of persons who admitted their fright to the AIPO interviewers is probably the very minimum of the total number actually frightened. Many persons were probably too ashamed of their gullibility to confess it in a cursory interview. On the other hand, people would not be so likely to prevaricate when asked whether or not they had heard the broadcast or whether or not they regarded it as news. But there is the possibility that some people heard so much about the broadcast that they reported actually hearing it.

Sectional differences in the reaction are not great except for the small percentage of New England listeners who were frightened. This is probably due to the fact that New England listeners had deliberately tuned in to a relatively remote station especially to hear *War of the Worlds,* since none of the large New England stations carried it. The higher percentage of fright among southern listeners may be due to the larger proportion of poor and uneducated people in this area.[7] The panic was clearly a nation-wide reaction. The figures below indicate the percentage of those who heard the broadcast as a news report and were frightened.

[7] For a discussion of the effect of economic status and education on the nature of a listener's reaction, see pp. 113 f.

*Sectional differences in extent of fright*

| | |
|---|---|
| New England | 40 per cent |
| Middle Atlantic | 69 |
| East North Central | 72 |
| West North Central | 72 |
| South | 80 |
| Mountain and Pacific | 71 |

*Reports of high school administrators.* Since it was thought that high school principals throughout the country would be in touch with a cross-section of the population and have some evidence of the extent of the reaction in their community, forms were mailed to every twenty-fifth school principal listed in state educational directories.[8] Of the 1044 questionnaires distributed, 305 or 29 per cent were returned. Thirty-nine per cent of the principals who answered reported that they knew of students in their schools who were frightened by the broadcast. They estimated that on an average about 5 per cent of their pupils were frightened. Since the questionnaires were obviously returned by the most interested administrators, it is difficult to estimate their representativeness. If we consider the number of children in school, it seems likely that approximately one quarter of a million children of high school age were upset by the dramatization.

*Telephone volume.* Accounts of frantic telephone calls flooding switchboards of radio stations, newspapers and police stations are confirmed by figures

[8] Although this method of selection covered the country thoroughly, it would not yield names in exact relation to the population distribution since fewer questionnaires were sent to the more urbanized states and to regions most advanced in consolidating rural schools. These objections, however, were not of sufficient importance for our purposes to justify a more elaborate, time-consuming sample.

secured from the American Telephone Company.[9] An increase of 39 per cent was reported in the telephone volume in metropolitan northern New Jersey during the hour of the broadcast as compared to the usual volume of that hour of the evening. A 25 per cent increase over normal in the same area occurred the succeeding hour. Increases for several suburban exchanges on Long Island for the same hours ranged from 5 to 19 per cent. In six suburban exchanges surrounding Philadelphia, traffic increased 9.6 per cent for the entire day of October 30 and for the entire New York metropolitan area traffic was above normal. Telephone officials see no other way to account for the increased volume than assigning responsibility to the broadcast.

The managers of the 92 radio stations that carried the broadcast were questioned by mail about their telephone volume during and immediately following the program. Of the 52 who replied, 50 reported an increase. Thirty-seven per cent noted increases of at least 500 per cent over the usual Sunday night volume; 31 per cent reported increases below 500 per cent. The others had no figures available. There seems little doubt then that a public reaction of unusual proportions occurred.

*Mail volume.* The interest the broadcast aroused is further shown by the number of letters written when it was over. Three-quarters of the station managers reported that their mail volume exceeded 100 per cent of the normal number of letters received. Several instances were reported of increases of over 500 per cent. Station WABC, Columbia's key station, was flooded with 1770

[9] The writer wishes to acknowledge the assistance of members of the Traffic Department in the New York office of the company for their assistance in gathering the data.

pieces of mail on this one subject, 1086 favorable, 684 unfavorable. The Mercury Theatre itself received 1450 letters concerning the program; 91 per cent congratulating them, 9 per cent condemning them. The Federal Communications Commission received 644 pieces of mail. Sixty per cent of the letters were unfavorable to the broadcast; 40 per cent favorable. These differences in the nature of the letters sent to the federal "watch dog of broadcasting" and to the producers are not surprising. They clearly indicate that those who wanted their protests taken seriously did not hesitate to communicate with the proper authorities, while those who appreciated good drama gave praise where praise was due.

*Newspaper clippings.* The opinion was frequently encountered the day after the broadcast that the general state of hysteria reported in the newspapers was merely an attempt to find good copy for papers on Monday morning when news is notoriously at low ebb. Even if we assume that less than 5 per cent of the population contributed to the reaction, this is hardly a legitimate suspicion. If something can excite 5 per cent of the population it *is* news. However, the figures above confirm the theory that there actually was something unusual and significant to report. Furthermore, the amount of newspaper space devoted to the episode for two weeks after the broadcast indicates a lingering fascination, although it cannot, of course, refute the charge that many accounts were embroidered to make good stories.

An analysis of 12,500 newspaper clippings appearing in papers throughout the country during the three weeks following the broadcast, reveals that, although the volume of press notices took the usual sharp decline the second and third days, considerable interest was maintained for five days and had not fallen below 30 per cent of the original volume by the end of the first week.[10] The trend is illustrated in Figure I. It can be seen that newspaper interest did not begin to flatten until the end of the second week. Notices were still con-

Figure I

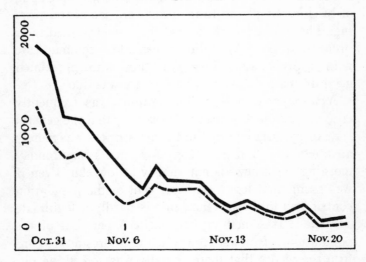

Solid line indicates number of newspaper items.
Broken line indicates number of newspapers containing items.

tinuing in appreciable volume when this analysis was made at the end of the third week. The increase of news items per paper at the outset is probably due to extra features, human interest and editorial comment.

There can be little doubt that this broadcast did affect a large number of people scattered throughout the coun-

[10] These clippings were collected from newspapers of every state by a reputable clipping bureau. The writer is indebted to the Mercury Theatre for generous permission to make full use of its files.

try. The problem for the psychologist now is to discover why so many people were frightened. This will require first an analysis of the broadcast itself. How was it actually experienced by the frightened listener? Why did he so readily confuse fiction with reality? The answers to these and other questions will occupy us in the next chapter.

*"It Didn't Sound Like a Play"*

# CHAPTER III ☼ HOW THE STIMULUS WAS EXPERIENCED

N O OTHER broadcast has produced a panic comparable to the one which found several million American families all over the country gathered around their radios listening to reports of an invasion from Mars. These reports were brought to them over a national network from New York City, our greatest metropolis, where people should know what is going on. Both the form and the content of the broadcast seemed authentic. As one listener put it "I just naturally thought it was real. Why shouldn't I?"

Even this program did not affect more than a small minority of the listeners. If we are to explain the reaction, then, we must answer two basic questions: Why did this broadcast frighten some people when other fantastic broadcasts do not? And why did this broadcast frighten some people but not others? An answer to the first question must be sought in the characteristics of this particular program which aroused false standards of judgment in so many listeners.

## Realism of Program

In spite of Dorothy Thompson's remark that "Nothing whatever about the dramatization was in the least credible, no matter at what point the listener might have tuned in,"[1] no one reading the script can deny that the broadcast was so realistic for the first few minutes that it was almost credible to even relatively sophisticated

[1] "On the Record," *New York Herald Tribune,* Nov. 2, 1938.

and well informed listeners (Miss Thompson excepted). The sheer dramatic excellence of the broadcast must not be overlooked.

This unusual realism of the performance may be attributed to the fact that the early parts of the broadcast fell within the existing standards of judgment of the listeners. By a standard of judgment we mean an organized mental context which provides an individual with a basis for interpretation. If a stimulus fits into the area of interpretation covered by a standard of judgment and does not contradict it, then it is likely to be believed. Just what some of the more accepted and common standards were that provided interpretations for the immediate acceptance of the broadcast as news are given below. Later in our discussion we shall be concerned with the problem of discovering more individualized standards of judgment which accounted for the persistence of the original interpretation even though the events reported became quite fantastic.

*Radio as accepted vehicle for important announcements.* The first wide use of radio in the country was to broadcast election returns. Since that time, important announcements of local, national and international significance have been repeatedly made. A few short weeks before this broadcast, millions of listeners had kept their radios tuned for the latest news from a Europe apparently about to go to war. They had learned to expect that musical programs, dramas, broadcasts of all kinds would be cut off in a serious emergency to inform or warn an eager and anxious public. A large proportion of listeners, particularly those in the lower income and educational brackets, have grown to rely more on the radio than on the newspapers for their news.[2] The confidence people have in radio as a source of news is shown in the answer to a question asked by the *Fortune* poll: "Which of the two —radio or newspaper—gives you news freer from prejudice?" Seventeen per cent answered "newspaper," 50 per cent believed radio news was freer from prejudice, while the rest either thought both media were the same, or didn't know which was less prejudiced.

On this particular night when the listener tuned to the Mercury Theatre, he heard the music of "Ramon Raquello and his orchestra" coming from the "Meridian Room" in the "Park Plaza Hotel" of New York City. Soon after the first piece had begun an announcer broke in "Ladies and gentlemen, we interrupt our program of dance music to bring you a special bulletin from the Intercontinental Radio News." With our present distance it is easy to be suspicious of "Intercontinental" news. But in the context of the program, such skepticism is reduced. This report brought the story of the first explosions on Mars. The music was resumed only to be followed by another break: "Ladies and gentlemen, following on the news given in our bulletin a moment ago, the Government Meteorological Bureau has requested the large observatories of the country to keep an astronomical watch. . . ." This bulletin contains the information that "a huge flaming object, believed to be a meteorite, fell on a farm in the neighborhood of Grovers Mill, New Jersey." The swing band gets in 20 seconds more. Then the invasion continues uninterruptedly.

[2] *Fortune,* Aug. 1939, p. 65. A thorough discussion of radio news broadcasting will be given in Paul Lazarsfeld, *Radio and the Printed Page,* now in preparation. (A publication of the Princeton Radio Project.)

Almost all of the listeners, who had been frightened and who were interviewed, mentioned somewhere during the course of their retrospections the confidence they had in radio and their expectation that it would be used for such important announcements. A few of their comments indicate their attitudes:

"We have so much *faith in broadcasting*. In a crisis it has to reach all people. That's what radio is here for."

"The announcer would not say if it was not true. *They always quote if something is a play.*"

"I always feel that *the commentators bring the best possible news*. Even after this I still will believe what I hear on the radio."

"It didn't sound like a play *the way it interrupted the music when it started.*"

*Prestige of speakers.* It is a well known fact to the social psychologist, the advertiser, and the propagandist that an idea or a product has a better chance of being accepted if it can be endorsed by, or if it emanates from, some well known person whose character, ability, or status is highly valued. The effect of this prestige suggestion is especially great when an individual himself has no standard of judgment by means of which he can interpret or give meaning to a particular situation that confronts him and when he needs or is interested in making a judgment or finding a meaning. The strange events reported by the announcers in this broadcast were so far removed from ordinary experience and yet of such great potential and personal significance to the listener that he was both bewildered and in need of some standard of judgment. As in many situations where events and ideas are so complicated or far removed from one's own immediate everyday experience that only the expert can really understand them, here, too, the layman was forced to rely on the expert for his interpretation.

The logical "expert" in this instance was the astronomer. Those mentioned (all fictitious) were Professor Farrell of the Mount Jennings Observatory of Chicago, Professor Pierson of the Princeton Observatory, Professor Morse of MacMillan University in Toronto, Professor Indellkoffer of the California Astronomical Society and "astronomers and scientific bodies" in England, France, and Germany. Professor Richard Pierson (Orson Welles) was the chief character in the drama.

When the situation called for organized defense and action the expert was once more brought in. General Montgomery Smith, commander of the State Militia at Trenton, Mr. Harry McDonald, vice-president of the Red Cross, Captain Lansing of the Signal Corps, and finally the Secretary of the Interior described the situation, gave orders for evacuation and attack, or urged every man to do his duty. It is interesting to notice that only the office of the Secretary of the Interior was named. Here the listener was affected entirely by the institutional rôle and status of an unnamed speaker. The institutional prestige of the other experts and authorities is obviously more meaningful and important than the individuals themselves.

This dramatic technique had its effect.

"I believed the broadcast *as soon as I heard the professor from Princeton* and the officials in Washington."

"I knew it was an awfully dangerous situation *when all those military men were there and the Secretary of State spoke.*"

"If so many of those astronomers saw the explosions they must have been real. *They ought to know.*"

*Specific incidents understood.* The realistic nature of the broadcast was further enhanced by descriptions of particular occurrences that a listener could readily imagine. Liberal use was made of the colloquial expression to be expected on such an occasion. The gas was "a sort of yellowish-green"; the cop warned, "One side, there. Keep back, I tell you"; a voice shouts, "The darn thing's unscrewing." An example of the specificity of detail is the announcement of Brigadier General Montgomery Smith: "I have been requested by the Governor of New Jersey to place the counties of Mercer and Middlesex as far west as Princeton, and east to Jamesburg, under martial law. No one will be permitted to enter this area except by special pass issued by state or military authorities. Four companies of State Militia are proceeding from Trenton to Grovers Mill and will aid in the evacuation of homes within the range of military operations."

Particularly frightening to listeners in the New Jersey and Manhattan areas were the mentions of places well known to them. The towns of Grovers Mill, Princeton, and Trenton, New Jersey were featured early in the broadcast; Plainsboro, Allentown, Morristown, the Watchung Mountains, Bayonne, the Hutchison River Parkway, Newark, the Palisades, Times Square, Fifth Avenue, the Pulaski Skyway, the Holland Tunnel, are all familiar to Jerseyites and New Yorkers. And listeners throughout the country would certainly recognize many of these names as real.

"When he said, 'Ladies and gentlemen, do not use *route number 23*' that made me sure."

"I was most inclined to believe the broadcast *when they mentioned places like South Street and the Pulaski Highway.*"

*"If they had mentioned any other places but streets right around here*, I would not have been so ready to believe."

*Everybody baffled.* The events reported proceeded from the relatively credible to the highly incredible. The first announcements were more or less believable although unusual to be sure. First there is an "atmospheric disturbance," then "explosions of incandescent gas." A scientist then reports that his seismograph has registered a shock of earthquake intensity. This is followed by the discovery of a meteorite that has splintered nearby trees in its fall. So far so good.

But as the less credible bits of the story begin to enter, the clever dramatist also indicates that he, too, has difficulty in believing what he sees. When we learn that the object is no meteorite but a metal casing, we are also told that the whole picture is "a strange scene like something out of a modern Arabian Nights," "fantastic," that the "more daring souls are venturing near." Before we are informed that the end of the casing is beginning to unscrew, we experience the announcer's own astonishment: "Ladies and gentlemen, this is terrific!" When the top is off he says, "This is the most terrifying thing I have ever witnessed. . . . This is the most extraordinary experience. I can't find words. . . ." A few minutes later, Professor Pierson says, "I can give you no authoritative information—either as to their nature, their origin, or their purposes here on earth. . . . It's all too evident that these creatures have scientific knowledge far in advance of our own. It is my guess. . . ." After the battle at Grovers Mill between the Thing and the soldiers, the announcer gives the listeners a final justification for the incredulous reports to follow: "I have a grave announcement to make. *Incredible as it may seem,* both the observation of science and the evidence of our eyes lead to the inescapable assumption that those strange beings who landed in the Jersey farmlands tonight are the vanguard of an invading army from the planet Mars."

The bewilderment of the listener is shared by the eyewitness. When the scientist is himself puzzled, the layman recognizes the extraordinary intelligence of the strange creatures. No explanation of the event can be provided. The resignation and hopelessness of the Secretary of the Interior, counseling us to "place our faith in God," provides no effective guide for action. No standards of judgment can be applied to judge the rapid-fire of events. Panic is inescapable.

*The total experience.* Careful observation of everyday life behavior or careful introspection of one's own reactions in the course of an ordinary day, indicate that in social life the normal individual experiences patterns or configurations of social stimuli. It is the "atmosphere" or the "effect" of a social situation that we notice long before we are able (if we happen to try) to analyze precisely what it is in the situation that creates the particular characteristic impressing us. The football fan, wedged in between enthusiastic alumni, listening to the bands and the shouting, watching the teams, has the experience of "being-at-a-football-game"—an experience which is, to be sure, composed of the various stimuli impinging upon him but an experience which results from the perception of all these stimuli as patterned, as coming-together, as being inextricably interwoven in the production of a *Stimmung* he may have travelled miles to experience. A person in church is likewise experiencing a social situation with particular characteristics that he can describe with adjectives meaningful to him. Even the "awe" or "deference" one may feel in an empty cathedral seems to be more of an immediate perception than an accretion due to a series of related, specific past experiences.

The importance of creating the proper atmosphere conducive to any desired action is, of course, well known to the revivalist, the cardinal, the dramatist, and, especially today, the dictator. The elaborate preparations made by Hitler and Goebbels for their national and party celebrations are recognized *musts* for them if they are to enlist the enthusiasm they want to demonstrate. It is obviously the total effect they are after, just as a composer keeps his whole theme in mind while writing separate bars of a symphony. The lights, banners, uniforms, airplanes, marching, singing, and speaking at Nüremberg congresses all go to make up the experience of a *Parteitag* and to reinforce adoration of *Der Führer*.

In our discussion we have broken the program down into what we regarded as important characteristics engendering belief. This type of analysis could easily be extended further by showing how individuals have been conditioned to more specific items in the drama. But the extension of this method puts a false emphasis on the problem by assuming at once that a social stimulus is essentially a series of discrete elements to which people have somehow learned to react. The enormously important possibility which our approach so far has overlooked is that social stimulus situations have their own characteristic and unique qualities. These qualities inhere in the total pattern or configuration of the stimulus, just as the characteristics of "triangularity" or "circularity" inhere in certain figures.

This broadcast of Martian invasion certainly had an "atmosphere" or structure all its own and the *methodological* device we have necessarily employed of describing one thing at a time should never obscure the fact that we are dealing with a situation *experienced as a unit*. For some persons, certain specific elements may have been more important in the total experience than others. The case studies show enormous variety. But no experience reported seems meaningful if entirely isolated from the whole context. The elementarism springs inevitably from the method of the investigation, not from the experience of the subject. If any one doubts this, let him reread the reactions reported at the beginning of the second chapter.

### Tuning in Late

In spite of the realism of the broadcast, it would seem highly unlikely that any listener would take it seriously had he heard the announcements that were clearly made at the beginning of the hour. He might then have been excited, even frightened. But it would be an excitement based on the dramatic realism of the program. There would not be the intense feeling of personal involvement. He would know that the events were happening "out there" in the studio, not "right here" in his own state or his own county. In one instance a "correct" (esthetically detached or dramatic) standard of judgment would be used by the listener to interpret events, in another instance a "false" (realistic or news) standard of judgment would be employed.

The number of listeners who dialed to the program after the preliminary announcement may be approximated by information obtained in two separate investigations. The data from each of these studies furthermore amply demonstrate that the time a person tuned in was a major determinant in shaping his later reactions.

In a special survey conducted for the Columbia Broadcasting System (CBS) the week after the broadcast,[3] interviews were made throughout the country on 920 persons who had listened to the broadcast. Among other questions asked were "At what part of the program did you tune in?" and "Did you realize it was a play or did you think it was a real news broadcast?" Forty-two per cent said they had tuned in late. And as Table 1 shows there was a very pronounced tendency for those who tuned in late to accept the broadcast as news, and for those who tuned in at the beginning to take it as a play. Only 12 per cent of the persons interviewed listened from the beginning and thought they were hearing a news report.

In the survey made by the American Institute of Public Opinion the question was asked "Did you listen from the beginning, or did you tune in after the program had begun?" Sixty-one per cent answered that they tuned in after the program had started, 35 per cent listened from the beginning, 4 per cent did not remember. As Table 2 shows, here again we find that those who tuned in late tended much more than others

[3] The writer wishes to thank the Columbia Broadcasting System for permission to analyze these data. Because of the time involved in making tabulations on the large number of cases, only half the sample was used (460 cases of the total 920). The sample was divided by the split-half method.

# TABLE 1

### TIME OF TUNING IN AND INTERPRETATION
### (CBS SURVEY)

| Interpretation | Tuned in | | Total Number |
| | From the Beginning (per cent) | After Beginning (per cent) | |
| --- | --- | --- | --- |
| News | 20 | 63 | 175 |
| Play | 80 | 37 | 285 |
| Total per cent | 100 | 100 | —— |
| Total number | 269 | 191 | 460 |

to regard the broadcast as news. Only 4 per cent of the sample tuned in from the beginning and believed the broadcast to be a news report.[4]

Both of these studies lead to the same conclusion: that tuning in late was a very essential condition for the arousal of a false standard of judgment. To be sure, many people recognized the broadcast as a play even though they tuned in late. Just why this was done and by whom will be discussed in the next chapter. But

[4] The percentage of persons in the CBS sample who thought the broadcast was news is noticeably larger than that in the AIPO sample. The difference may be due to several conditions. For one thing, the CBS survey was made within a few days after the broadcast when respondents were well aware that many other people had been similarly fooled and when they might, therefore, have been more willing to confess their own mistakes. Furthermore, the AIPO sample represents the whole population, whereas the CBS interviewers, instructed to question any listeners they could find, were more likely to be attracted to people who were known to have listened because of their exciting experiences.

It will also be noticed that the CBS sample contained a much larger proportion of persons who listened from the beginning. It is difficult to explain this difference in a satisfactory way. The people questioned by the AIPO interviewers may have forgotten the very beginning because of the more outstanding events which they remembered and which were reported later in the broadcast. The CBS survey was more rigorous and elaborate and would seem more accurate on this point.

## TABLE 2

TIME OF TUNING IN AND INTERPRETATION
(AIPO SURVEY)

| | Tuned in | | |
| Interpretation | From the Beginning (per cent) | After Beginning (per cent) | Total Number |
|---|---|---|---|
| News | 11 | 35 | 104 |
| Play | 89 | 65 | 267 |
| Total per cent | 100 | 100 | —— |
| Total number | 134 | 237 | 371 |

for our present purposes it is important to raise and to answer the question of how anyone who tuned in at the beginning could have mistaken the clearly introduced play for a news broadcast.

Analysis of these cases reveals two main reasons why such a misinterpretation arose. In the first place, many people who tuned in to hear a play by the Mercury Theatre thought the regular dramatic program had been interrupted to give special news bulletins. The technique was not a new one after their experience with the radio reporting of the war crisis in October 1938. And it was a more usual procedure to accept such news reports as irrelevant to the expected program than as an integral part of it. Of the 54 persons in the CBS survey who listened from the beginning and thought the broadcast was a news report, 33 (61 per cent) said that the interruption seemed to them authentic. This is apparent from the comments:

"I have heard other programs interrupted in the same way for news broadcasts."

"I believed Welles's statement that he was interrupting the program for a news flash."

"The news was presented in such an authentic manner."

The other major reason for the misunderstanding is the widespread habit of not paying attention to the first announcements of a program. Some people do not listen attentively to their radios until they are aware that something of particular interest is being broadcast. Since the beginning of the hour is concerned with station identifications and often with advertising, it is probably disregarded. About 10 per cent of the 54 people who misinterpreted the broadcast although they heard it from the beginning said they had paid no attention to the announcements. These people obviously just happened to be tuned to the Columbia station and were not, like the others who erred, anticipating the Mercury Theatre.

"My radio had been tuned to the station several hours. I heard loud talking and excitement and became interested."

"My radio was tuned to the station but I wasn't paying attention to it."

"We had company at home and were playing cards while the radio was turned on. I heard a news commentator interrupt the program but at first did not pay much attention to him."

"I started to listen only when the farmer began giving a description of the landing of the tube."

Anyone who studies the characteristics of radio knows that one of its chief shortcomings is its inflexibility as far as time is concerned. The listener must be at his dial at the right moment if he is to hear the program. In this respect print obviously enjoys an enormous advantage.[5] Newspapers, magazines and books can be read when it is convenient to read them, whereas a radio program exists for a few brief minutes and then disappears forever. The broadcaster can point out, however, that comparatively few people do much reading.

This disadvantage of radio has many practical consequences for the advertiser, the politician, or the educator. The advertiser does not want to send his expensive commercial announcement into an air thinned of potential customers. The clever politician does not want to waste his best oratory before he has attracted the greatest possible audience. The late Huey P. Long, well aware of the radio habits of his constituents, began one of his radio talks as follows: "Friends, this is Huey P. Long speaking. I have some important revelations to make but before I make them I want you to go to the phone and call up five of your friends and tell them to listen in. I'll just be talking along here for four or five minutes without saying anything special, so you go to the phone and tell your friends that Huey Long is on the air."

The great bulk of the latecomers consists of people who either turn their dials casually at the beginning of the hour trying to find something that pleases them or of people who intended to listen to a specific program when it began but misjudged the time. The CBS survey showed that two-thirds of those who had tuned in late did not know what program they wanted to hear as they turned their dials, while 12 per cent of the late-

[5] cf. Paul Lazarsfeld, *op. cit.*

comers had actually intended to listen to the Orson Welles broadcast at the beginning.[6]

Tuning in late, then, is a normal aspect of the listening situation. But now we discover that tuning in late may lead to mass hysteria. Such a phenomenon is so far rare but might conceivably become important in times of crisis or national emergency. In such situations it may be necessary to use different techniques to give news or information, perhaps wording a report in such a way that late listeners could understand it without becoming frightened. This problem is important for our purposes now since we must discover why approximately 50 per cent—an unusually high proportion— of the listeners to this broadcast tuned in late, as the combined figures of the American Institute and the CBS surveys reported above seem to indicate.

The large percentage of listeners who tuned in on this special occasion after the program had begun seems chiefly due to two reasons. In the first place, it must be remembered that the Mercury Theatre program was competing with the most popular program of the week, that of the versatile, wooden hero, Charlie McCarthy. The regular weekly survey of Hooper, Inc., a commercial research organization checking on the audiences of programs, estimated the ratio of listeners to Orson Welles and Charlie McCarthy as 3.6 to 34.7. According to restricted "meter-checks" the average family listens 48 minutes out of the 60 minutes to the

[6] On the other hand, if the listener has some favorite program to which he is faithful or if he is eager to hear a special broadcast, then he may frequently tune to the proper station early to make sure that he does not miss anything. If an educational program is followed directly by a popular variety show, it inevitably enlarges its audience during the last few minutes. If a program has the good fortune to precede a boxing match, it may double its audience.

Charlie McCarthy program. Since McCarthy and his stooge Bergen were the recognized features of this competing broadcast, it seemed probable that some people who did not listen throughout the whole hour would either turn off their radios when the dummy act was finished or would cruise around on the dial until they found something that interested them. If many persons did this, it is likely that they would misunderstand the nature of the Welles broadcast and keep their sets tuned to that program to learn more about the situation being so vividly described.

To check this possibility, 846 cards were sent to persons all over the country known to have listened to the Mercury Theatre broadcast. They were asked if at any time during the hour they had heard the Charlie McCarthy program and, if so, had they tuned out when Charlie McCarthy had finished his first act. Cards were returned by 518 persons. Eighteen per cent reported that they had heard the competing program and 62 per cent of these said they had tuned out when McCarthy had finished his first act and that they had then kept their dials set to Orson Welles. The excitement of the Martian invasion then apparently stopped the dials of about 12 per cent of Charlie McCarthy's devotees.

A second important reason for the increase in the number of late arrivals was the contagion the excitement created. People who were frightened or disturbed by the news often hastened to telephone friends or relatives. In the survey made by the American Institute of Public Opinion all people who tuned in late were asked "Did someone suggest that you tune in after the program had begun?" Twenty-one per cent said "Yes."

In a special telephone study made for CBS by Hooper, Inc., it was found that 15 per cent of the 103 persons interviewed had tuned in late to the program because they were telephoned to do so; in the CBS survey 19 per cent were found to have listened after the beginning because others told them to hear the news.

Tuning in late to this broadcast was, then, partially due to a well known radio habit and partly to the fact that the program was sufficiently exciting either to keep some listeners fixed to this program or to stimulate other listeners to tell their friends to listen to the strange reports. In any event, tuning in late was very decisive in determining whether or not the listener would follow the program as a play or as a news report. For the story of the Martian invasion was so realistic that misinterpretation was apt to arise without proper warning signals.

*"We'd Better Do Something"*

# CHAPTER IV ☼ DESCRIPTION OF REACTIONS

IN SPITE of the fact that many persons tuned in late to hear this very realistic broadcast, by no means all of them believed it was news. And not all of those who thought the invasion was upon them behaved the same way in the face of danger. Before we can understand the reasons for the varying behavior, the reactions must be arranged in some significant grouping. Otherwise no fruitful conceptualization is possible.

Our ultimate aim in explaining the behavior is to understand the reasons for the panic. The validity of our understanding could only be tested if we were in a position to predict on the basis of it what people would become panicky during a comparable event. Since another invasion from Mars seems unlikely in the near future, we can test our final explanation only by means of the adequacy with which it accounts for the variety of behavior our investigations have uncovered. And as we begin to classify our data in order to understand them better, we are of course already making an hypothesis. Such a procedure is inevitable. Yet the rationale behind any classification finally adopted needs some justification.

From correspondence, interviews, and newspaper clippings we have information concerning the reactions of hundreds of people. These reactions could be grouped in many ways. We could, for example, differentiate between people who ran out of their houses, and those who did not, people who listened to the whole broadcast and those who tuned out. But such classifications would probably reveal little of final psychological significance. At first it seemed most reasonable to distinguish between people who were frightened, disturbed, or calm in their reactions to the broadcast. This distinction proved very useful as we shall see later. But it became clear that one important psychological factor was not included in such a division: the degree of intelligent behavior displayed in the panic situation. If some people were frightened because they believed the broadcast implicitly while others remained frightened after they tried somehow to establish the authenticity of the news reports, then a separation of frightened and non-frightened listeners obscured an important source of information.

The classification which finally brought the data together in a way to yield greatest understanding was based strictly on the behavior exhibited by the persons interviewed. It has four categories and presupposes that all the persons at first thought the broadcast was a news report.

1. Those who analyzed the internal evidence of the program and knew it could not be true.

2. Those who checked up successfully to learn that it was a play.

3. Those who checked up unsuccessfully and continued to believe it was a news broadcast.

4. Those who made no attempt to check the authenticity of the broadcast.

This grouping not only tells us about the way a given individual reacted but also something of his intentions and capacities. It gives us a story of the process and function of the behavior. We can learn something of the beginning and end of the reaction by analyzing the orientation made. It thus describes a type of activity with which we should be able to relate a maximum number of the characteristics to be found in the listener himself. The classification was derived from analysis of the 135 detailed interviews.

## Classifying the Listeners

1. *Those who checked the internal evidence of the broadcast.* The persons in this category were those who did not remain frightened throughout the whole broadcast because they were able to discern that the program was fictitious. Analysis of the reactions of the listeners in this category clearly reveals two major reasons for the independent judgments they were able to make.

About half of these people detected the broadcast as a play because of some specific information they possessed and were able to project into this situation. Several listeners soon related the story to H. G. Wells. A few had read *War of the Worlds.*

"I turned the radio on to get Orson Welles, but the announcement that a meteor had fallen sounded so much like the usual news announcements that I never dreamt it was Welles. I thought my clock was probably fast. . . . When the machine started to come apart *I couldn't imagine what it was,* but when the queer forms began to come out *it flashed over me suddenly* that this *was* the Orson Welles program, and I remembered that it was called *The War of the Worlds.*"

Others recognized Orson Welles and immediately relaxed.

". . . when things began to come out I was already in the habit of believing the beginning and I kept right on believing. . . . I just was carried away by the realistic method of production. I was swept along with it *until something started to sound familiar*. It was Orson Welles, of course! I felt awfully foolish, especially when I thought back and saw how fantastic even the little I did believe was."

Some realized that the reports must be false because they sounded so much like certain fiction literature they were accustomed to.

"At first I was very interested in the fall of the meteor. It isn't often that they find a big one just when it falls. But *when it started to unscrew and monsters came out, I said to myself, 'They've taken one of those Amazing Stories and are acting it out.'* It just couldn't be real. It was just like some of the stories I read in *Amazing Stories* but it was even more exciting."

"For a second when I heard that smoke was spreading I thought it might be a fire. *It sounded so fanciful* —using terms like 'people dropping like flies.' Then I also wondered where could the announcer be so as to be able to describe this thing and not be affected by it. It went so fast—within a couple of minutes, smoke and gas spread miles. It couldn't possibly spread so fast. I listened for about a minute and said, *'That sounds like a Buck Rogers story.'* "

One listener had been in the army and knew that there were not three regiments of infantry in the vicinity which could be rushed to the scene of the disaster. "So," he said, "I knew the broadcast must be a hoax."

The other half of the persons who can be placed in this category are those who believed the reports for a short time but could not take seriously the descriptions of subsequent events. There was too apparent a contradiction between what they were hearing and what they knew for sure was possible.

"It all sounded perfectly real *until people began hopping around too fast* . . . when people moved 20 miles in a couple of minutes I put my tongue in my cheek and figured it was just about the smartest play I'd ever heard."

". . . I heard the announcer say he was broadcasting from New York and he saw a Martian standing in the middle of Times Square *and he was tall as a skyscraper.* That's all I had to hear—just the word Martian was enough even without that fantastic and incredible description. . . . I knew it had to be a play."

"I kept translating the unbelievable parts into something I could believe *until finally I reached the breaking point—I mean my mind just couldn't twist things any more,* and somehow I knew it couldn't be true literally, so I just stopped believing and knew it must be a play."

2. *Those who checked the broadcast against other information and learned that it was a play.* These listeners tried to orient themselves for the same reasons as those in the first group—they were suspicious of the "news" they were getting. Some simply thought the reports were too fantastic to believe; others detected the incredible speeds revealed; while a few listeners checked the program just because it seemed the reasonable thing to do. Their method of verifying their hunches was to compare the news on the program to some other information. The most common means of checking employed by listeners in this group was the easiest and most obvious—to see if other stations were reporting the invasion. Over half of the group did this and were

satisfied. A few others supplemented this procedure by looking up the program in the newspaper. Some checked only by referring to the paper. One person called up a friend and another looked out the window.

"I thought it might be a play although I cannot give any reason why I thought so. It was so real. But *I turned to WOR to see if they had the same thing* on and they didn't so I knew it must be a fake."

"I tuned in and heard that a meteor had fallen. Then when they talked about monsters, I thought something was the matter. *So I looked in the newspaper* to see what program was supposed to be on and discovered it was only a play."

3. *Those who tried to check the program against other information but who, for various reasons, continued to believe the broadcast was an authentic news report.* Two characteristic differences separated the people in this group from those who made successful checks. In the first place, it was difficult to determine from the interviews just why these people wanted to check anyway. They did not seem to be seeking evidence to test the authenticity of the reports. They appeared, rather, to be frightened souls trying to find out whether or not they were yet in any personal danger. In the second place, the type of checking behavior they used was singularly ineffective and unreliable. The most frequent method, employed by almost two-thirds of this group, was to look out the window or go outdoors. Several of them telephoned their friends or ran to consult their neighbors. A few telephoned the police or a newspaper office. Only one turned his radio dial. Only one consulted a newspaper.

There are several reasons why the checks made by these persons were ineffectual. For some of them, the new information obtained only verified the interpretation which their already fixed standard of judgment provided.

"I looked out of the window and everything looked the same as usual *so I thought it hadn't reached our section yet.*"

"I went outside once to look at the stars. I saw a clear sky but *somehow was not reassured.*"

". . . I ran to look out the window and *I didn't see anything, so I thought it hadn't reached our section yet.*"

". . . I went to the window and looked over to New York. I *didn't see anything unusual there either, so I thought they hadn't gotten there yet.*"

For others the observed data were interpreted as additional evidence that the broadcast was true.

"I was alone with my two younger brothers. My parents had gone to a party in Newark. When they mentioned 'citizens of Newark, come to the open spaces,' I got scared. I called my mother to find out what to do and *there was no answer.* I found out later that they had gone to an empty apartment so that they could dance. Nobody was left at the place I phoned. My only thought was that the flames had overcome my parents."

"We looked out of the window and Wyoming Avenue was black with cars. *People were rushing away, I figured.*"

"No cars came down my street. *'Traffic is jammed on account of the roads being destroyed,' I thought.*"

"My husband tried to calm me and said, 'If this were really so, it would be on all stations and he turned to one of the other stations and there was music. *I retorted, 'Nero fiddled while Rome burned.'* "

"We tuned in to another station and heard some church music. *I was sure a lot of people were worshiping God* while waiting for their death."

"I stuck my head out of the window and thought I could smell the gas. And *it felt as though it was getting hot, like fire was coming.*"

"I looked out of my window and *saw a greenish-eerie light* which I was sure came from a monster. Later on it proved to be the lights in the maid's car."

Other listeners were unable to trust their own observation, believing that other people knew more about the situation than they did.

"I was listening with my son—I had tuned in a little after eight. At the beginning it was not here so I was not scared. But when the gas came nearer the boy started crying. I was terribly upset. I looked out of the window where we can see the airport, but I did not see anything. But then the announcer said: 'Everybody go up on their roofs,' I felt *it was his function to warn us against things* we were not aware of, so I took my boy and rushed upstairs. In passing I warned the neighbors on the higher floors. I was so terribly upset that they tried to calm me—they phoned the police and found out that it was all a play."

"I was home and my friend called and said, 'is your radio working? Tune in WABC—the world is coming to an end.' I tuned in and heard buildings were tumbling down in the Palisades and people were fleeing from Times Square. I could hear the noise in the radio *and the announcer said so.* It was not static but things actually falling, so I did not get up and look out. *He would know it being right there.* So I just listened."

"My sister, her husband, my mother and father-in-law were listening at home. I immediately called up the Maplewood police and asked if there was anything wrong. They answered, '*We know as much as you do. Keep your radio tuned in and follow the announcer's advice. There is no immediate danger in Maplewood.*' Naturally after that I was more scared than ever. I became hysterical and felt I was choking from the gas. We all kissed one another and felt we would all die. When I heard that gas was in the streets of Newark I called my brother and his wife and told them to get in their car and come right over so we could all be together."

"We were called up to tune in because something terrible was happening. I went right to the telephone and called my married daughters. I told them not to leave, we would call for them. I looked out of window, but could not see anything. My son came home during the excitement and *I sent him out to find one of the elders* in the church to see what it was all about."

4. *Those who made no attempt to check the broadcast or the event.* It is usually more difficult to discover why a person did *not* do something than why he did. Consequently it is more difficult for us to explain why people in this group did not attempt to verify the news or look for signs of the Martians in their vicinity than it was to determine why those who attempted unsuccessful checks displayed their rather aimless behavior. Over half of the people in this group were so frightened that they either stopped listening, ran around in a frenzy or exhibited behavior that can only be described

as paralyzed. From an analysis of the interviews we can roughly place the people in this category into several groups according to the apparent reasons for their actions.

a. Some of them reported that they were so frightened they never thought of checking.

"We were so intent upon listening that we didn't have enough sense to try other hook-ups—*we were just so frightened.*"

"We didn't try to do anything to see if it were really true. *I guess we were too frightened.*"

b. Others adopted an attitude of complete resignation. For them any attempt to check up, like any other behavior, appeared senseless.

"I was writing a history theme. The girl from upstairs came and made me go up to her place. Everybody was excited I felt as if I was going crazy and kept on saying, 'what can we do, *what difference does it make* whether we die sooner or later?' We were holding each other. Everything seemed unimportant in the face of death. I was afraid to die, just kept on listening."

"I tuned in when the weather reports were given. I was with my little boy. My husband was at the movies. *I thought it was all up with us.* I grabbed my boy and just sat and cried. And then I could not stand it any more when they said they were coming this way. So I turned the radio off and ran out into the hall. The woman from next door was out there crying too."

"I didn't do anything. I just kept listening. I thought *if this is the real thing you only die once*—why get excited?"

"The lady from the next floor rushed downstairs, yelling to turn on the radio. I heard the explosion, people from Mars, end of world. I was very scared and everybody in the room was scared stiff too. *There was nothing to do* for everything would be destroyed very soon. If I had had a little bottle of whiskey, I would have had a drink and said, 'let it go.' "

c. Some felt that in view of the crisis situation, action was demanded. A few prepared immediately for their escape or for death.

"I couldn't stand it so I turned it off. I don't remember when, but everything was coming closer. My husband wanted to put it back on but I told him *we'd better do something instead of just listen,* so we started to pack."

"We had turned in to listen to Orson Welles but when the flashes came I thought it was true. We called my brother who had gone out. He said he would be right down and drive away with us. When he came we were so excited. I felt why can the children not be with us, if we are going to die. Then I called in to my husband: 'Dan, why don't you get dressed? You don't want to die in your working clothes.' My husband said we were here for God's glory and honor and it was for Him to decide when we should die. *We should prepare ourselves.*"

Several people were occupied in caring for hysterical co-listeners or in warning relatives or friends.

"We were having an anniversary party and I happened to tune in a little after eight—there were special bulletins—a great ball had landed and militia and police rushed to the place—creatures were popping up and down and the police could not come near because they were burned by the terrible heat. I really did not listen much because *I was so busy rushing around.*

My sister had left her children alone at home. She almost went crazy. I tried to get a taxi for her but our phone was being used by so many excited guests."

"I was visiting the pastor's wife when a boy came and said, 'some star just fell.' We turned the radio on—we all felt the world was coming to an end. I felt if the gas was on I wanted to be with my husband and my nephew so I ran out of the house—I stood on the corner waiting for a bus and *I ran out to every car* thinking it was a bus. When I got home my husband was not there so *I rushed to the neighbors to tell them* the world was coming to an end. Then I woke up my nephew. Finally my husband came home about eleven o'clock. We turned on WOR and they said it was a play."

Certain respondents believed that the safest thing to do was to remain constantly tuned in to the broadcast to learn just when and how they should escape.

"We happened to tune in incidentally. A terrible thing was happening and the militia was called. There was nothing we could do about it and *they told us to stay tuned in.* It seemed most important to follow them."

"A friend called me around 8:15. She was so excited that I thought I had better see for myself. *I did not do much of anything except listen.* I thought of going out in the car to see what was happening but then I felt it would not do me much good. I felt switching stations was useless; if it was a maniac as I believed, the other stations might not have it."

d. Some listeners interpreted the situation in such a way that they were not interested in making a check-up. In a few instances the individual tuned in so late that he missed the most incredible parts of the program and was only aware of the fact that some kind of conflict was being waged.

"I was in my drugstore and my brother phoned and said, 'Turn the radio on, a meteor has just fallen.' We did and heard gas was coming up South Street. There were a few customers and we *all began wondering where it could come from.* I was worried about the gas, it was spreading so rapidly but I was puzzled as to what was actually happening, when I heard aeroplanes I thought another country was attacking us."

"I had the idea that it was either an eruption of natural gas or an explosion with fire. I thought *whatever it was* it was the most extensive catastrophe ever having happened in New Jersey. I was really scared—my sister was in Newark at a party and I feared she got caught in it. *I never thought of the Martians. I did not hear that part.* I was just going to call my mother to see whether she had heard from my sister when the announcement came."

Occasionally individuals would reconstruct the event from their own points of view to make what was apparently fantastic more credulous.

"I happened to tune in when the meteor had just fallen. I did not know how I finally found out. I never believed it was anyone from Mars. I thought it was some kind of a new airship and a new method of attack. *I kept translating the unbelievable parts* into something I could believe. I felt a good deal was the announcer's imagination but something was behind it."

"At first I was not frightened—happened to tune in rather early. Then when the gas was spreading I got scared. I thought they were trying to keep the worst away from people yet they wanted them to know something was wrong. *I thought they might not know themselves completely what it was."*

*"I knew it was some Germans trying to gas all of us.* When the announcer kept calling them people from Mars *I just thought he was ignorant* and didn't know yet that Hitler had sent them all."

For others the events described did not involve immediate personal danger.

"I was at a party, somebody was fooling around with the radio, and we heard a voice, the Secretary of the Interior was talking. We thought it was a normal bulletin because of the conditions abroad. Then the local militia was called so we decided to listen. It sounded real but not like anything to get panicky about. This riot or whatever it was *was still a couple of miles away."*

"I listened from the very beginning. I always listen to the Mercury Theatre. But when the flashes came I thought they were really interrupting the play. I did not look for other stations because they said it was the only one not destroyed. We looked at the sky but could not see anything. I was not very upset though because *we were in as safe a place as possible*—high up, and the higher you are the safer you are from gas fumes."

*Exceptional cases.* If some listeners who tuned in late displayed no actual behavior as a result of the broadcast, they obviously cannot be included in the present classification. But since the orientation to the broadcast involved emotional as well as strictly behavioral reactions, the listeners we have omitted in our classification must by no means be discarded. Later on

(Chapter VI) the persons who have not been considered in the present discussion because their behavior in the situation was thwarted by external circumstances will be studied separately and will furnish new clues regarding additional factors which affect adjustment in a panic situation. Our classification of the listeners who tuned in late to the broadcast and thought it was a news report therefore includes every one of the 135 cases interviewed except 34 people whose reactions never fully developed because of some situational circumstance and two cases which were so anomalous that they could not be fitted anywhere. Twenty-eight of these persons had checks made for them by other people. Hence their own typical behavior was interrupted. Some reports of these instances will show how the information was relayed and the reactions changed.

"When I heard the militia was wiped out, I went downstairs and listened. At first I didn't think there was any danger. A monster in a pit had fallen from somewhere and took life and shape. Then later I heard Martians and realized the creatures were from Mars. I didn't realize at first that they were hostile—my impression was that communication with Mars was beginning. In a short time I realized that these creatures were attacking. It wasn't beyond a possibility that such things could happen, but it seemed peculiar that the announcer could be right next to it and watching it. When the creatures began to come nearer here *my sister's friend called his brother who told him it was a play.*"

"First we thought something was happening down in Princeton, some meteor had fallen, and some catastrophe was developing. So we just listened. But then it got nearer—the gas was spreading. I wanted to take the car and get out to be safe. *Just then a friend of mine came in,* she knew the voice of Welles."

Six of the remaining cases could not be classified under our categories because the people made checks accidentally and quite unintentionally by moving their dials.

"My dial on the radio was set high and *when I turned to WABC I passed other stations and I heard music on the other stations.* I felt if anything was wrong it would be on all stations, so I grabbed the newspaper and saw *The War of the Worlds* was being broadcast."

*"We turned to other stations not because we had any doubts* about the authenticity of the broadcast but we wanted to hear what other commentators had to say. Perhaps they had different reports. Of course, we got the usual programs on the other stations and we turned back to hear the broadcaster starting to choke and saying he would stay to the end and he was the last station on the air and we realized it was a play because the other stations were still on the air."

"I happened to stand up and *I happened to knock the radio.* It is an old and easily tuned radio and the knock changed the station and I heard music and I felt if something was actually happening it would be on all stations and I felt it must be a play."

## · *Numerical Orientation*

If we can get some idea of the proportion of listeners who reacted in the four characteristic ways we have described, we shall have a more definite frame of reference for understanding the whole panic situation. There are two sources of information: the 99 detailed interviews we have been able to place in our classification and the CBS survey. Of the 460 persons interviewed in this latter study, 175 thought the broadcast was news and of these 24 learned the real nature of the broadcast by coincidence or by the checks of others so that it is impossible to tell how they might have reacted if left to their own resources. The 151 remaining cases are available for classification.

In comparing the data from these two investigations the differences between them must be borne in mind. The persons for whom case studies were made were not chosen because they were in any way representative of the listening population: we deliberately sought out more people who were frightened. Furthermore, all of these interviews were made in a restricted area centering around northern New Jersey. The CBS interviews were much more representative. The interviewers commissioned by Columbia were instructed to question any people they could find who had listened to the program. Their sample had a national coverage. Our case studies were made several weeks later than the CBS interviews. On the other hand, our interviewers were more highly trained psychologically and the information they were asked to obtain was much more detailed. In brief, the CBS survey is more accurate in terms of its sampling, while our case studies are more thorough and psychologically revealing.

In spite of these differences, the classification of listeners from the two surveys shows surprisingly similar results (Table 3).

TABLE 3

PROPORTION OF LISTENERS IN THE FOUR REACTION
GROUPS AS OBTAINED FROM TWO SETS OF INTERVIEWS

| Reaction Groups | Case Studies (per cent) | CBS Survey (per cent) |
|---|---|---|
| 1. Successful internal checks | 23 | 20 |
| 2. Successful external checks | 18 | 26 |
| 3. Unsuccessful external checks | 27 | 6 |
| 4. No checks attempted | 32 | 48 |
| Total per cent | 100 | 100 |
| Total number | 99 | 151 |

This table shows that over one-third of the people who first tuned to the broadcast as news and were not informed of their error by some other person or by some accident failed to make any checks whatsoever. Approximately one-fifth of them tested the authenticity of the program by analyzing its intrinsic qualities. While among those who tried to check with reference to some other information, about half were successful and half unsuccessful.[1]

[1] The discrepancies between the distributions obtained in the two surveys can be reasonably explained by the differences between the studies. The low percentage of unsuccessful checks noted in the nation-wide sample is undoubtedly due to the fact that such checking behavior would hardly be recorded in a brief interview. Such behavior as looking out the window or calling a friend are subtle details that a condensed interview would likely neglect. Such persons were probably listed among those who made no attempt to check, thus producing the disproportionately larger percentage of listeners in the fourth category under the CBS survey. The greater number of persons classified from the rougher interviews as belonging to the group which made successful checks is probably due to the fact that, without careful analysis, persons who were told of the play by friends or who made other unintentional checks would be listed among those who checked successfully.

*Behavior and feeling.* It is common knowledge that when people are very excited, worried, or afraid they are less likely to react intelligently than when they are calm. The champion boxer learns to keep his head no matter how severe his opponent's blows; the successful airplane pilot is the one who maintains his composure while weathering a storm; the good soldier is the one who carries out the command no matter how great the danger. And in everyday life, the harassed individual is the one more apt to make foolish mistakes. The story goes of a man who had been forced to let his car stand out for several hours in sub-zero weather. He was sure that it wouldn't start when he returned. He tried it and his fears were confirmed—until he discovered he had not turned on the ignition switch. In Chapter IX, we shall discuss this problem at greater length. But it is important for our purposes now to discover just how the people we have classified in our four categories felt during the supposed invasion. Analysis of the case studies and the CBS survey will show us the relationship.

The 99 detailed interviews were classified by two independent judges into three groups: frightened, disturbed, and calm. The following method was used in distinguishing between the degrees of excitement: first, all persons who clearly were not affected by the broadcast were separated from the total sample, then persons whose reactions or reports of their feelings at the time pointed to unequivocal fright were combined, leaving a third group which was neither calm nor very frightened and which we classify broadly as "disturbed." The agreement between the judges' ratings was very high

$(r = .95)$. The CBS respondents were similarly rated but only by one person.

Table 4A shows that of those people in the case studies who made unsuccessful checks or no checks at all, every one was at least disturbed, whereas none of the people who were able to check the intrinsic character of the broadcast was really frightened. On the whole we may conclude that those who checked successfully, either by internal or external tests, remained fairly calm, while those who checked unsuccessfully or not at all tended to become excited. This general conclusion is confirmed by a similar study of the CBS data. (Table 4B.)[2] The data from both investigations indicate the relationship between behavior and feeling.

## TABLE 4A

### RELATION OF BEHAVIOR AND FEELING
#### (CASE STUDIES)

| | | Behavior | | | |
| Feeling | Internal checks (per cent) | Successful external checks (per cent) | Unsuccessful external checks (per cent) | No checks (per cent) | Total per cent |
| --- | --- | --- | --- | --- | --- |
| Frightened | 0 | 11 | 67 | 65 | 39 |
| Disturbed | 48 | 33 | 33 | 35 | 37 |
| Calm | 52 | 56 | 0 | 0 | 24 |
| Total per cent | 100 | 100 | 100 | 100 | 100 |
| Total number | 23 | 18 | 27 | 31 | 99 |

[2] Although the same relationship between feeling and behavior is shown in both sets of data, the total percentage of persons classified in the three groups according to fright show rather striking differences. The CBS study indicates that one-half the people were frightened, whereas only about one-third of the case studies showed definite fright. This difference is probably not due to the nature of the samples but to the fact that the CBS survey was made more immediately after the broadcast when people would be more likely to admit their fright than they would later.

RELATION OF BEHAVIOR AND FEELING
(CBS SURVEY)

| Feeling | Internal checks (per cent) | Behavior | | | Total per cent |
| | | Successful external checks (per cent) | Unsuccessful external checks (per cent) | No checks (per cent) | |
|---|---|---|---|---|---|
| Frightened | 26 | 59 | 89 | 70 | 60 |
| Disturbed | 52 | 39 | 11 | 27 | 33 |
| Calm | 22 | 2 | 0 | 3 | 7 |
| Total per cent | 100 | 100 | 100 | 100 | 100 |
| Total number | 31 | 39 | 9 | 22 | 151 |

Since the purpose of our investigation was not to determine the degree of fright but the reasons for it, these differences in amount of fright are not important. In both sets of data, the *relationship* between fright and behavior remains the same.

We have now differentiated the reactions to the realistic stimulus of the broadcast into what would seem to be the most appropriate categories. We have found out what proportion of the persons who tuned in to this program as a news broadcast fitted into each of our four groups. We have also learned that the persons who were frightened were in general those who failed to make adequate checks. The next problem is to discover what there is about a person that determines into which of the four groups he will fall.

*"I Figured"*

# CHAPTER V ☼ CRITICAL ABILITY

HERE was a broadcast which frightened some people but not others. What was it that made some people interpret the program correctly even though they tuned in late? Of all the possible psychological capacities and characteristics individuals possess, what ones would we expect from our data and our present knowledge to be most helpful in giving us a better understanding of this panic situation? We might choose frustration, repression, introversion, egocentrism or any one of dozens of conceptualizations we know are important to the psychologist. But since the panic arose essentially from an error in judgment, it seemed most likely that the factors which we should look for would be those which helped listeners judge such a situation correctly.

People who were fundamentally skeptical and unwilling to jump at conclusions would presumably be likely to examine the evidence in this case before accepting the announcer's reports. Such people who habitually scrutinize interpretations before accepting them would be apt to know how to go about the self-imposed task of verifying the information heard on this program. Other people might judge the program to be a play because they had certain special knowledge or training which they were able to relate to the broadcast and to use as a frame of reference for their own orientation. Psychologically, persons who for either of these reasons detected that something was wrong can be said to have had "critical ability." By this we mean that they had a capacity to evaluate the stimulus in such a way that they were able to understand its inherent characteristics so they could judge and act appropriately.

## Critical Ability and Education

This critical ability is a promising single psychological tool with which to examine our data. But there is no direct way to measure it. No applicable psychological tests exist. So it was necessary to see what information gathered would probably be most closely related to critical ability. The most likely index obtained seemed to be the amount of formal education a person had. For theoretically, at least, education instills a readiness to examine interpretations before accepting them and at the same time gives people a certain fund of information which should provide useful pegs for their own evaluations.

*Education and Orientation toward the Broadcast.* An analysis of the CBS survey with education as the index yields gratifying results. It shows that only about half as many people with a college education, as compared to those with a grammar school training, believed the broadcast was a news report (Table 5).

## TABLE 5
### EDUCATION AND INTERPRETATION AS NEWS
### (CBS SURVEY)

| Education | Percent who thought program was news report | Total number of cases |
|---|---|---|
| College | 28 | 69 |
| High school | 36 | 257 |
| Grammar school | 46 | 132 |

But two other factors might conceivably cause this high correlation. We know that in the United States today younger and wealthier people are better educated. Therefore age and economic status must be examined before we can safely conclude that education is the fundamental determinant.

When the interpretations which people above and below forty years of age placed on the broadcast are studied, the importance of education as a determinant remains unchanged: in both age groups more highly educated people were more frequently able to recognize the broadcast as a play (Table 15, Appendix C). Education also holds its place when people in different economic strata are separately compared: as education decreases, misinterpretation increases for persons in high, average, and low income brackets (Table 14, p. 157).

In many surveys the economic status of persons is known but information concerning their educational backgrounds is lacking. Therefore economic status must frequently be taken as a substitute index for education. When listeners are grouped for comparative purposes by income alone, persons in the lower income category tend to accept the broadcast as an authentic news report more frequently than persons in the higher levels (Table 6). This result, however, has only a descriptive value. We should expect that inasmuch as poorer people are less well educated they would be more likely to misinterpret the broadcast. But we have found in addition that there is a tendency for people with low education to misinterpret the broadcast *irrespective* of their economic status.[1]

[1] The result of the above analysis of the CBS survey when respondents are grouped by economic status, is corroborated by the data obtained in the

## TABLE 6

### ECONOMIC STATUS AND INTERPRETATION AS NEWS
### (CBS SURVEY)

| Economic status | Proportion interpreting program as news report | Total number of cases |
|---|---|---|
| High | 35 | 240 |
| Average | 37 | 152 |
| Low | 49 | 66 |

Education is also found to be influential in enabling people to check on the authenticity of the program after they are told that it is a news broadcast. When the 99 case studies already classified according to the type of check made are further grouped by educational level, we discover that two-thirds of those who made successful checks were high school graduates while only one-half of the people who failed to check or who checked unsuccessfully completed high school. Table 7 shows in detail the relationship of education to the various orientations.

nation-wide survey of the AIPO. Twenty-seven per cent of their respondents who were in the high economic bracket interpreted the program as a news report as contrasted to 36 per cent of the people in the low income group. It seems reasonable to expect that this difference would have been greater had it been possible to classify the AIPO sample by education. But unfortunately no question concerning education was included in this survey.

It should be pointed out that the use of education as a more significant index than economic status is obviously limited to those areas of interest and judgment where income would not seem to play any decisive rôle. For example, when people are asked whether or not they approve of President Roosevelt's policies, economic status is found to be much more closely related to their opinions than education (Table 16, Appendix C).

In general a correlation of about .80 may be expected between education and economic status if foreign born groups are excluded from the sample. For the theory of this procedure and further illustration, see Paul Lazarsfeld, "The Interchangeability of Indices," *Jl. Appl. Psychol.*, 1939, 23, 33-46.

TABLE 7

REACTION TO BROADCAST ON DIFFERENT
EDUCATIONAL LEVELS

| Education | Successful internal checks | Successful external checks | Unsuccessful external checks | No checks attempted | Total |
|---|---|---|---|---|---|
| More than high school | 14 | 7 | 11 | 5 | 37 |
| Completed high school | 4 | 2 | 3 | 10 | 19 |
| Completed grammar school | 5 | 8 | 13 | 16 | 42 |
| Not ascertainable | — | 1 | — | — | 1 |
| Total | 23 | 18 | 27 | 31 | 99 |

*The nature of critical ability.* The original problem was to determine the relationship between critical ability and reactions caused by the broadcast. Listeners have been divided according to their educational backgrounds in lieu of a more direct psychological measure. Now we can distinguish between four groups of people:

| Education | Most successful orientation | Least successful orientation |
|---|---|---|
| High school or more | 1(+) | 2(—) |
| Less than high school | 3(—) | 4(+) |

The expected tendency is that listeners will fall into the "plus" boxes: that educated people will orient themselves successfully while uneducated people will not make the proper interpretation. Although this was the trend we found it was by no means what invariably happened. But before we consider the deviate cases, we should examine the 27 people who had more than high school education and who oriented themselves properly to the broadcast (those in box 1 above) to see what we can learn about the structure of critical ability.

First of all, why did educated people so much more than relatively uneducated discover from internal evidence that the program was a play after all? About half of them found the broadcast simply too fantastic to believe. Their reports show that they were able to call upon certain standards of judgment which they thought were trustworthy. When these were uncompromisingly contradicted, especially by Martian monsters, they dismissed the program as untrue.

"I kept believing and disbelieving at the same time. *I believed in the possible parts according to my knowledge,* but disbelieved as soon as I heard about monsters and tentacles."

*"It sounded plausible until they announced that creatures began to appear.* Then it sounded very fantastic and we realized it was a story. The part about the creatures hopping about and growing taller was too fantastic."

"I heard the announcer say he was broadcasting from New York and he saw a Martian standing in the middle of Times Square and he was as tall as a skyscraper. *That's all I had to hear*—just the word Martian was enough even without fantastic and incredible description."

Some persons were sufficiently sure of their interpretations to think that the announcer was making a mistake.

"I thought the 'unscrewing' of the top of the meteor was the *announcer's hallucination* and that the thing was just disintegrating."

"I figured *the announcer was excited and made a mistake.*"

The other half of the educated groups had sufficient specific knowledge to recognize the dramatic character of the broadcast. Some were familiar with Wells's story; others could tell that Orson Welles was playing the rôle of Professor Pierson: one person knew that there were not so many national guardsmen in the vicinity and another person riding in the midst of the devastated area saw no signs of disaster. This division between those who recognized the broadcast as fantastic and those who had special knowledge suggests that critical ability results either from a general capacity to distinguish between fiction and reality or the ability to refer to special information which is regarded as sufficiently reliable to provide an interpretation.

The next problem is to find out how education is related to the reasons for and the methods of making checks against information not already possessed or obtained from the program itself. Altogether 45 people tried successfully or unsuccessfully to check the broadcast against outside sources. Persons with superior education tried, more than others, to verify the program against information which would itself be less likely to be colored by the suggestion that Martians were rampant in the East. Newspaper listings of radio schedules and programs coming from other stations would not be affected by a scary play, whereas friends and neighbors might.

TABLE 8

TYPE OF CHECKS MADE BY PERSONS IN DIFFERENT
EDUCATIONAL GROUPS

| Type of check made | Educational Level | |
| --- | --- | --- |
| | High school or more | Less than high school |
| Looking outdoors | 10 | 8 |
| Turning radio dial | 9 | 4 |
| Consulting newspaper | 6 | 3 |
| Calling friend | 1 | 5 |
| Calling official | 2 | 1 |
| Other or not ascertainable | — | 1 |
| Total number of checks | 28 | 22 |
| Total number of persons | 23 | 21 |

The value of these different checks to the listeners may be seen when the amount of credence placed in each type is studied (Table 9). An especially poor check was that of looking outdoors: only one of the 18 persons who did this believed such a check after he had made it. On the other hand, the confirmations of the program made by turning the radio dial or consulting the newspaper proved most reliable and were, as we have found, the checks most frequently used by the more educated listeners. Thus the most convincing checks and those which eventually led to a proper orientation to the broadcast were of the type most often made by people in the higher educational group.

From this discussion of the characteristic reactions of educated people who correctly judged the broadcast, we may draw certain conclusions regarding the nature of critical ability. Any one or any combination of several distinctive psychological processes seem to be involved.

## TABLE 9

### TYPE OF CHECK MADE BY ITS RELIABILITY
### TO LISTENER

| Type of check made | Believed checks | Did not believe checks |
|---|---|---|
| Looking outdoors | 1 | 17 |
| Turning radio dial | 11 | 2 |
| Consulting newspaper | 7 | 2 |
| Calling friend | 2 | 4 |
| Calling official[2] | — | 3 |
| Other or not ascertainable | — | 1 |
| Total number of checks | 21 | 29 |
| Total number of persons | 18 | 27 |

A person may have a predisposition to doubt interpretations until he has been able to verify them for himself according to knowledge he already possesses or information he feels is reliable. Or a person may not be habitually suspicious but may happen to have some knowledge which he refers back to and which shows him discrepancies between what he knows to be true and what a stimulus suggests.

### Deviate Cases

Not all educated persons remained calm or made successful checks, while some uneducated persons soon recognized the broadcast as a play. Formal education, then, is not an unfailing index of critical ability. Or perhaps critical ability alone is insufficient protection for some people against panics. If the cases which de-

[2] This apparently reliable check proved unsatisfactory in these instances since in two cases the officials themselves were perplexed and in the other case the telephone lines were so busy the call could not be completed.

viate most from the general correlation between education and successful evaluation are analyzed we should discover more about critical ability or the circumstances under which it can operate.[3] In Table 7, based on the 99 case studies classified by education and orientation there were five people with less than high school training who were successfully able to check the broadcast without recourse to outside information (those in box 3 of our diagram) and 15 people with more than a high school education who made no checks at all and were frightened or disturbed (those in box 2). These people are the most atypical of all.

*Persons with little formal education who recognized the broadcast as a play.* Thumbnail sketches of the five people in this group must suffice to show something of their personalities and the circumstances which led to their reactions.

1. A little girl of eleven, still in grammar school, was given special permission to stay up late to listen to Orson Welles whom she had previously heard as *The Shadow.* She was, therefore, not surprised to find him doing something else fantastic and she probably recognized his voice. She reported that "it sounded very real where they said 'We now take you to the farm.' But we knew it was a play."

2. A young Italian of twenty-three believed the events reported until "the creatures came out of the machine. Events were too fast from then on to be real." He is a sensitive man who reads serious literature and has mature interests. He is handicapped by a

[3] The general procedure employed here of studying cases that deviate from an expected trend was suggested by Lazarsfeld and has been used by him in *Radio and the Printed Page.*

poor environment, inadequate educational background, and backward parents.

3. A young man of twenty-five who knew it couldn't be real because "it was just like some of the stories I read in *Amazing Stories.*" This judgment was confirmed by his conviction that men could not come from Mars *yet* and by his checks on the impossible speed with which events transpired.

4. A calm woman of fifty-five who "never thought for a moment that it was anything but a play. It was so fantastic and far-fetched. Sounded like an enlargement of Buck Rogers—just like the Funnies."

5. A self-educated carpenter now sixty-two years old. He has a keen mind, likes academic arguments and is able to discuss social, scientific, and political trends intelligently. He seems to have an excellent general background for which his grammar school education is a completely inadequate index.

All of these deviate cases still point to the fact that critical ability was the most important factor enabling people to react appropriately. About half of these persons with less than high school terms recognized the broadcast because of specific knowledge and half because of a critical attitude gained through self-education and alert minds. There is some indication that personality factors may be important—the "calm" woman and the "sensitive" young man. But what we chiefly find in these case studies is corroboration of our common knowledge that formal education itself is not the only determinant of critical ability. Native intelligence, general interests, personality traits, or special information may all serve as better substitute indices of critical ability for certain people who have not had educational advantages.

*People with high formal education who made no checks.* What are the influences which militated against the operation of critical ability in the 15 people who had at least graduated from high school? Analysis of the interviews on these people reveals at least four reasons why the expected trend was not invariably found.

In the first place, the term "high formal education" is a very vague one used only as a rough substitute for critical ability. In addition to the simple distinction between amount of education, there is the less tangible factor concerning the quality of education. The graduate of an up-to-date city high school may have had a very different training than the graduate of a backward school in an underprivileged community. The result is that at times any distinction between a high school graduate and a person with less than high school training becomes tenuous indeed. Furthermore, anyone knows that all graduates of the same high school emerge with enormously different critical abilities. For these reasons, among others, our rough index may misplace certain people. For example, one high school graduate who failed to check at all was a young man in whom no signs of intellectual interest could be detected. He read no books, magazines, or newspapers and listened only to swing music on the radio. It took him seven years to finish high school. But in spite of these qualifications concerning education as an index, it should be pointed out that no college graduate who failed to check the program was found in our small sample. We know from other data that some college people did fail to check and were frightened. But the chances are that critical ability is very widespread among people who have survived advanced schooling.

A second reason why some of the educated people failed to verify the program was because they happened to tune in when relatively plausible reports were being given. They did not know about the Martians. The stimulus was not originally experienced by them as something utterly fantastic.

"You see, *all I heard was* that there was gas and that people were being killed and that the highways were jammed."

"*I heard something about poison gas* and people jumping into the Hudson River."

If these had been persons of a higher educational level, they might, to be sure, have been suspicious even of what they did hear.

In the third place, for many of these 15 relatively well-educated people unusual listening situations seemed to counteract whatever critical ability they may normally have possessed. Some were told to tune in by frightened persons; others experienced a stimulus which included not only the broadcast but the reactions of frightened people in the environment; while others were provided confirmatory checks on the reality of the broadcast by accidental circumstances. These influences seemed particularly noticeable among persons who were the best educated in this selected group. Here is one example. The respondent was a trained nurse who was having a party in her house.

"Everybody was terribly frightened. Some of the women almost went crazy. The men were a little calmer. Some of the women tried to call their families. Some got down on their knees and prayed. Others were actually trembling. My daughter was terribly frightened and really suffered from shock. A ten-year old child that was here was petrified. He looked like marble."

A final reason for the failure of some educated people to attempt any checks is found in certain characteristics of their personalities. The respondents' answers to questions about their beliefs, worries, wants, outstanding concerns and prides indicated attitudes and traits which made them prone to accept the broadcast as true.

This review of the 15 people who had at least finished high school and who made no attempts to check the authenticity of the broadcast points to at least two other factors which must be examined more thoroughly before our analysis of the panic is complete: characteristics in the personality of the listener himself and characteristics in the listening situation. The next chapter tells in greater detail how each of these factors contributed to false interpretations, how each seemed somehow to submerge critical ability in this particular situation.

*"I'm So Worried"*

# CHAPTER VI ☼ CONDITIONS INHIBIT-
## ING CRITICAL ABILITY

THE day after the Martian invasion explanations for the strange events were rampant. And, as usual, such explanations made by persons who were not frightened and who felt it their business to pronounce on such matters, attributed the panic to certain inherent characteristics of persons who got excited. Dorothy Thompson, columnist, blamed the "incredible stupidity" of the victims; a prominent psychologist said that no "intelligent" person would be taken in; another claimed that the disturbed people were all neurotic. Such glib generalizations are not only wrong but dangerous, both theoretically and socially. They attribute the explanation to a stimulus that automatically arouses people of a certain "type" and they thus obscure the underlying contexts we have already found so important; they presuppose that we do not need to look for further explanation; they condemn "the masses" in wholesale fashion.

In the previous chapter we have suggested that "critical ability" is an accurate description of the most important single psychological variable related to the panic reaction. This critical ability is not likely to be a simple innate capacity that some people have and others do not have. Its genesis in the individual is the result of a particular environment which has played upon his particular capacities. Whenever critical ability could function we discovered that it was complete insurance against panic behavior. But critical ability *alone* was not always sufficient insulation. At least two other factors were often so prominent in the picture that critical ability was blotted out. The first of these influences concerned some characteristic of the listener's personality, the second related to the nature of the actual listening situation in which the listener found himself when he tuned in to the broadcast.

### Personal Susceptibility

Everyday experience tells us that people of more or less similar educational backgrounds and analytical abilities do not all act alike in a critical situation. Some people lose their heads, others show self-control. Less intellectualized characteristics of their personalities come into play, cut across critical ability, and affect it for better or for worse. Our impressionistic study of the deviate cases has already indicated that this was the case with certain listeners. But can we find more clear-cut evidence to confirm our impression?

The ideal procedure would be to give a number of people who listened to the broadcast a battery of personality tests and see what characteristics emerged in those people who were well educated but still frightened.[1]

[1] Three standardized tests were actually administered to 30 frightened persons: the Otis Self-Administering Tests, Higher Education, Form A to measure intelligence, the Willoughby Personality Schedule designed to measure neurotic tendencies, and the Pressey X-O test to measure the range of emotional response. The scores of the frightened persons were compared to the published norms for the first two tests and to results obtained from a control group in the Pressey Test. Although completely negative results were obtained, no conclusions can be drawn from these data because difficulties of administration made it impossible to select ahead of time an adequate or representative sample of frightened listeners. The difficulties encountered suggest that whenever investigators are studying a comparable problem and intend to use such tests, it would be advantageous to give the tests to a sample of persons who are chosen *after* other data have been partially analyzed. In this way the factors supposedly measured by these tests can be more systematically related to known behavior.

But such an approach is impossible. In the first place, any test of a personal capacity or trait assumes that it is found in all members of the population and that its variation is quantitative but not qualitative. Experience of everyday life as well as psychological studies should convince us that even such an apparently uniform capacity as "intelligence" has personalistic dimensions completely neglected when any given person takes a test that has been standardized for a large population. What is true of intelligence is probably even more true of expressive, attitudinal, or temperamental traits. Hence any attempt to discover fundamental relationships between such capacities or traits and such a unique reaction as that aroused by the Martian invasion would seem to have limited value.

And even if we could assume, for a moment, that some trait or traits were uniform in the population, what ones should we choose to relate to panic behavior? Psychologists have listed almost 18,000 words in the English language describing behavior.[2] "Introversion" is one of these words. It is a psychological concept for which we have several tests. But there is no particular reason to expect introverts to be chiefly in the frightened or the calm reaction groups: their introspections might lead them to be either more independent in their judgments or more sensitive to impending dangers. "Submissiveness" is another trait we can roughly measure, but why should submissive persons react uniformly in this situation? One submissive soul may, to be sure, be overpowered by the authoritative reports he hears but

[2] cf. G. W. Allport and H. S. Odbert, "Trait-names: a Psycho-lexical Study," *Psychol. Monog.*, 1936, No. 211. See also Gordon W. Allport, *Personality: a Psychological Interpretation*, Chaps. IX-XVI, for a critical discussion of the elements of personality and testing procedures.

another, because he is submissive, may be an habitual radio fan or a voracious reader and thus have more specific knowledge to give him relevant standards of judgment.

And as we have already pointed out, such terms as introversion and submissiveness are likely to be blanket concepts obscuring enormous differences between persons whose introversion or submissiveness is only partially alike. If we choose such characteristics as "neuroticism" or "emotional instability" we have even more difficulty in defining precisely what we mean. For such terms, though frequently useful for purposes of general description, can easily become wastebasket concepts for anything that is not related to critical ability. Furthermore, what tests there are for these dispositions are apt to be *potpourris* of loosely related items found revealing in the measurement of a variety of more specific traits.

From analysis of our data it seemed that the general characteristic of personality that made people vulnerable to the broadcast was what we might call susceptibility-to-suggestion-when-facing-a-dangerous-situation. The word "susceptibility" must be so qualified if it is to carry the exact meaning intended. A single word is inadequate. This susceptibility we should expect to be due to complex interaction between the unique temperaments of single individuals and their equally unique environmental backgrounds. Although it may lead different persons to similar behavior, its multiple genesis makes it difficult to define and to measure precisely. Furthermore, even if we did have an instrument to tap the degree of susceptibility to suggestion when facing a critical situation, the instrument would have to be much more highly refined than most personality tests now in use if it were to distinguish between the various groups of people we have classified in our small sample of 99 case studies.

A more realistic and appropriate measure than that provided by any test was devised by Lazarsfeld.[3] It consisted essentially of measuring a factor of personality by pooling different bits of information all of which seemed to point to a single prominent characteristic. By consciously reconstructing the intuitive process, an impressionistic procedure was transformed into a quantitative method. Knowledge of seven different kinds revealed by the interview schedule seemed likely to be particularly indicative of susceptibility.[4]

1. *Insecurity.* Knowledge of this factor was obtained from the following questions on the interview schedule: "Is the security of your job dependent on business conditions or the friendship of certain people?"; "What are the things in your life which you would like to have different?"; and "What are the things you worry most about?"

Here are some typical replies to these questions.

[3] The method was originally developed in another study of the Princeton Radio Project to ascertain an individual's "reading standard." cf. Paul Lazarsfeld, *Radio and the Printed Page.* This general procedure gives quantitatively reliable results which may often be overlooked in case studies. Rather than lose valuable information it is possible to emphasize it.

[4] In some interviews, there were 11 possible criteria for susceptibility but information on four of these was incomplete in many instances and could therefore not be used in our tabulations. Obviously if we had been able to construct our theory more adequately before we undertook the study we might have obtained better criteria and made sure that all information was complete. The four incomplete criteria omitted were: belief in science, outstanding concern when involved in the catastrophe, racial prejudice, and chronic nervousness.

"My husband has a job in a Federal Symphony orchestra but *for the last 10 years he has had no steady work.*"

"*I haven't been employed for four years* on account of the depression and *I don't know how long my brother's job will last.*"

"*I'd like to have more of a chance* to learn things. Then I might be able to live in a better place and Ma wouldn't have to worry so much."

"I'm so worried about my looks. I wish I were better looking. *It's time I was getting married* but the boys I like never like me."

"As you see I'm a colored man. My color is against me wherever I turn. *I can't get as good a job as I think I deserve* and no matter how hard I try *certain positions are closed to me* and I have to live, work, and play where the white folks dictate."

2. *Phobias.* This criterion was based on the answer to the question "What three things are you most afraid of?" A wide variety of specific phobias was found in the respondents—fear of death, high places, falling, crossing streets, water, noises, being home alone, stairs and many others. Again a few examples must suffice.

"I lived through an earthquake in Austria and *explosions of any kind scare me.*"

"While I was on my wedding trip I *almost got drowned.* I was scared to death."

"Twenty years ago I *saw lightning strike* the ocean and divide the water. I felt it came from heaven and this broadcast reported things just like that."

3. *Amount of worry.* Information here was gathered from the question, "Do you consider that you worry more than other people?" The respondents indicated

whether they felt they worried more, less, or about the same amount as others.

4. *Lack of self-confidence.* This characteristic was judged from answers to a question taken directly from the Allport Ascendance-Submission Reaction Study. The question dealt with an individual's readiness to argue with someone in public. The alternate answers are found in the interview schedule (Appendix B).

5. *Fatalism.* Because a person who resigns himself to mysterious powers beyond his control can rationalize any experience as preordained, he would appear to be particularly susceptible to the belief that he was faced with a catastrophe when he heard the broadcast. This attitude was obtained from the questions "Does man's life on this earth seem to you meaningless, temporary or futile?"; "What did you do when you thought the broadcast was true?"; and "What sort of a catastrophe did you think it was?"

"I just kept listening. I thought if this is the real thing you only die once—why get excited. *When the time comes you go and there is no getting away from it.*"

"*I believe what is to be will be.* I didn't pray during the broadcast."

"My husband took Mary into the kitchen and told her that *God had put us on this earth for his honor and glory* and that *it was for Him to say when it was our time to go.* Dad kept calling 'O God, do what you can to save us.'"

6. *Religiosity.* This information was chiefly gathered from spontaneous elaborations to the question, "Do you believe that God can and does control events on this earth?" A simple "yes" answer did not, of course,

classify a person as unusually zealous but the question led many persons to digress on their eschatological beliefs.

"We just sat and listened. You see we're good Christians and *a Providence will take care of us*. We're not afraid to die because *we're prepared* for it."

"At first I didn't think it was the end of the world because I read in the Bible, in Revelations, that *the end of the world was coming by fire* and I didn't think this was a fire. I thought buildings were being struck and falling down. But then I realized that eventually they might catch on fire so I thought the end was coming."

"*The Bible says* that the first time the end of the world was by flood and *the next time it will be* by fire and that went through my mind."

7. *Frequency of church attendance.* Listeners were asked to state whether or not they went to church frequently, occasionally, or never. This was taken as a rough measure of religious interest since more detailed information of the respondent's religious beliefs made it impossible for us to rate him on some such scale as fundamentalism-liberalism. Since a large proportion of people undoubtedly go regularly to church in order to participate in a social event or to receive intellectual stimulation, this is certainly by no means always an index of an individual's belief in and worship of a Higher Power controlling man's destiny.

*Evidence.* Each case was classified according to these criteria. A person was given a plus if it was felt that he definitely fell into a category, a minus if he definitely did not, and a zero if it were doubtful. The number of plus signs opposite an individual provided a measure of his susceptibility.[5] The work-sheet appeared as follows:

| Interview number | Insecurity | Phobias | Worries | Lack of self-confidence | Fatalism | Religiosity | Church attendance |
|---|---|---|---|---|---|---|---|
| 1 | + | + | 0 | — | 0 | + | + |
| 2 | — | + | + | — | 0 | — | — |
| 3 | — | — | — | — | — | 0 | + |
| 4 | + | — | — | + | + | + | + |

How is susceptibility as obtained in this fashion related to the different reactions to the broadcast and to education which we have found so indicative of critical ability? Table 10 indicates that persons who successfully oriented themselves were less susceptible to suggestion on this occasion. It also shows that educated people were less susceptible than relatively uneducated people. If this statistical result were otherwise, we should immediately have to suspect it. But much more important for our present purposes is the fact that the differences between the vulnerability scores are much greater *within* each educational group than they are between the educational groups.[6] This clearly indicates

[5] Such a procedure is, to be sure, subjective. But a misjudgment on any one of seven subvariables would be much less serious than a misjudgment on the whole variable itself. Furthermore errors in judgment undoubtedly tended to cancel each other.

[6] Table 18, Appendix C, analyzes in more detail the type of orientation made by persons in different educational level.

that our original distinction between the different orientations is valid and that we have here a measure of a characteristic of personality that is not by any means wholly dependent on educational background.

TABLE 10[7]

DIFFERENCES IN SUSCEPTIBILITY INDEX OF BEHAVIOR GROUPS IN DIFFERENT EDUCATIONAL LEVELS (PROPORTION OF POSITIVE INDICATIONS OF SUSCEPTIBILITY)

| Education | Successful orientation | Unsuccessful orientation |
|---|---|---|
| High school or more | 21 | 36 |
| Less than high school | 24 | 41 |

Some psychologists may object to this procedure and say that we still know nothing about general susceptibility to suggestion in the face of a dangerous situation and that all we know is how people who showed seven separate patterns of behavior reacted in relation to this broadcast. They would argue that the assumption of a general characteristic of "susceptibility" is merely an unscientific reification of a bundle of actually discrete elements of personality we happened to find related. This argument—contrary as it is to common sense and to evidence—is too involved to answer here completely.[8]

[7] Wherever the term "successful orientation" is used it indicates the combined reactions of those whom we have formerly designated as having made successful internal or external checks. Similarly the term "unsuccessful orientation" refers to persons who checked unsuccessfully or not at all. The numbers upon which Table 10 was based will be found in Table 17, Appendix C. In Table 18 of the same appendix another method of analysing the data is explained. The same results appear.

[8] Any interested reader will find a detailed discussion of this psychological problem in Allport, *op. cit.*, or H. Cantril, "General and Specific Attitudes," *Psychol. Monog.*, 1932, No. 192.

But it does force us to justify our procedure and to speculate on the nature of this particular characteristic of personality we find so important.

Whether or not an individual will reveal any one of the beliefs, anxieties, or behavior patterns which we have used as our seven criteria will depend to a large extent upon his background as well as his innate temperament. A person obviously must be in an environment potentially capable of affecting him in a certain way if he is to be so affected. Some persons might worry about economic insecurity if they had not inherited a trust fund or acquired a steady job, others might be intensely religious if they had been brought up in fundamentalist homes, others might develop phobias if they had suffered traumatic experiences. But still not all people who lack economic security, who were taught the literal truth of the Old Testament, or who have had dangerous escapes seem to show signs of undue susceptibility in critical situations. We must infer that some predisposition has operated as a selective force so that some persons are consistently impressed by experiences which leave others unaffected. This particular pattern of sensitivity and the characteristic behavior it determines is a general personality trait.

All of the seven criteria we have used refer to an individual's behavior and beliefs before the broadcast of the invasion. And because of the variety of experience different people have, we should not expect that all the persons in our case studies would be marked positive on any single criterion. But we should expect that these chance factors, resulting from different backgrounds, would cancel each other out so that when we pool the criteria together under one concept we would get some significant result. This is precisely what happens. No single criterion alone shows a significant statistical trend. But when taken together the trend is clear cut in spite of the small number of cases. All of these criteria, then, point to a more generalized personality trait which is, by definition, a consistent mode of response to a variety of situations.

But what is this trait? What is the similarity of relationship between the individual and each of these seven criteria we at first intuitively selected? What more general subjective relationship between the individual and his world is indicated by analysis of insecurities, phobias, worries, lack of self-confidence, fatalism, religiosity, and frequency of church attendance? In the first place, each implies a certain feeling of personal inadequacy. The individual is unable to rely on his own resources to see him through. He feels relatively helpless and believes his own best efforts at a better adjustment are insufficient. This means, furthermore, that the individual believes his life and his fate are very largely dependent on some forces outside himself—on chance, on economic conditions far beyond his control, or on the whim of some supernatural being. All this adds up to an intense feeling of emotional insecurity, one which is likely to be augmented as the situation surrounding the individual appears more and more threatening. His own standards of judgment either predispose him to regard his efforts as inadequate or dependent on outside forces or else his emotional insecurity makes him lose faith easily in any appropriate standards he may have. The net result is that the individual will be highly susceptible to suggestion when he is face-to-face with a situation that taxes his own meager self-reliance. His emotional insecurity is pervasive and dynamic. It steers his judgment and behavior. The events reported by this broadcast clearly threatened personal security, called for personal resourcefulness, and confidence in personal evaluations. Our analysis has demonstrated that these combine into a trait of personality which must be definitely regarded as an additional factor to be used in explaining the panic.

Whatever critical ability a person may normally have, it is ineffective if in any given situation his emotional insecurities are so great that they overwhelm his good judgment. Such situations are likely to be those where the individual himself or something dear to him are threatened. The immediacy and the intensity of the forces around him are such that they stimulate and sustain his low threshold of susceptibility to suggestion before his critical ability can come into play.

### The Listening Situation

For many people who listened to the broadcast the radio reports were by no means the only stimuli in the total listening experience. Some people heard their telephones ring and answered to find that excited friends were telling them to tune in to the broadcast, others listened with older relatives, others with friends whom they were visiting, others in public places, others alone at home separated from their loved ones. The total listening situation was probably somewhat different for each listener. And when we remember that the listening situation, like most other social stimuli, is a complex pattern which tends to be experienced as a unit and not as a series of discrete elements, then we realize the enormous variety of stimulus-configurations different listeners were exposed to. Each configuration would tend to influence the listener in a particular way. Some of them probably were of such a nature that they tended to dull normal critical ability. In examining some of the possible psychological consequences of these different listening situations, we shall not look for a uniform cause as we did in our analysis of personality. The wide variety of possible listening situations would make such a search absurd.

*Some characteristics of listening situations.* What are some of the influences aside from the broadcast itself that may have been important in determining the listener's reaction to the program?

One of the things we would first suspect is *the corroboratory effect of other people's behavior: the contagion of other people's fear.* A person who was told to tune in by a frightened friend would listen under different conditions than someone who tuned in for other reasons. If the person who called him was someone whom he had confidence in, he would be particularly apt to accept that person's opinion, tune in with a pre-existing mental set, and have his attitude confirmed.

*"My sister called up and I immediately got scared. My knees were shaking."*

"I was resting *when an excited person phoned* and told me to listen to the radio, that a big meteor had fallen. I was really worried."

Some listeners who were told to tune in by frightened individuals might doubt the authenticity of the report. But when they turned on their radios and then, sure enough, heard what they had been told they would hear, they might lose their original skepticism.

"I had just gone to the store to get some last-minute things for my daughter's party. When I came in my son said, 'Mother, something has come down from Mars and the world is coming to an end.' I said, 'Don't be silly.' *Then my husband said, 'It is true.' So I started to listen.* And really, I heard 40 people were killed and there was gas and everybody was choking."

Certain people who were mildly disturbed or suspicious were so surrounded by the excited reactions of others that their ordinary critical abilities were hampered.

"I was alone in police headquarters, when someone phoned me and asked what was happening on the radio. I turned it on and just happened to hit the right station. Gee, did I get scared. *I tried to check by calling the station but the lines were busy, and then more people started calling and they kept on calling,* so I was listening to the radio with one ear and the telephone with the other. I did not get any chance to phone outside. I kept telling people it was nothing to worry about, that it was only a story but I was only trying to quiet them and all the time I was talking, the sweat was pouring down my face, because I was so scared, and I was cussing out the other cops for leaving me alone. But I had to stay. I did not have time to turn to another station, and was sure relieved when I heard what it really was."

"I don't think we would have gotten so excited *if those couples hadn't come rushin' in the way they did.* We are both very calm people, especially my husband, and if we had tuned in by ourselves I am sure we would have checked up on the program but *they led me to believe it was any station.*"

Sometimes the sight and sound of other people who were frightened might increase the emotional tension of an otherwise relatively calm individual and thus reduce his critical ability.

"When I came out of the telephone booth, the store was filled with people in a rather high state of hysteria. I was already scared but *this hysterical group convinced me further that something was wrong.*"

"I was getting worried when my friend came in and *his face was ghastly white.* He said, 'We're being invaded,' and *his conviction impressed me.*"

Sometimes listeners may be upset by other people, not because their impressions were corroborated, but merely because of *the disturbing effect of other people* upon them. We know that for some individuals the tumult of a group, especially if its members are excited, somehow retards their intellectual activity.[9] They like to be alone or at least in a quiet place when they must reason something out. They are unable to concentrate with so many distracting stimuli around them. This effect may have been particularly apparent in some instances, since the broadcast occurred on a Sunday evening when people were normally relaxed.

"My wife kept outwardly calm too. But *there were so many people around that neither of us had a chance to collect our wits* and see what was really the matter."

"I was in a grocery store and *customers bothered me so that I couldn't find out* for awhile what other stations had on."

[9] cf. J. F. Dashiell, "Experimental Studies of the Influence of Social Situations on the Behavior of Individual Human Adults," in *A Handbook of Social Psychology* (edited by C. Murchison), Worcester: Clark University Press, 1935, Chap. XXIII.

Another influence that might have varied the nature of the listening situation was *the listener's status in a group*. If a person is usually the dominant member of a group, we should expect that the reactions of other people would not particularly impress him. But if he plays a usually more submissive rôle in a certain social situation because of his age, his subordinate position, his knowledge, or his characteristic deference, then he would be more apt to imitate and believe the reactions of his superiors.

"My mother took my word for it because *after all I was a college graduate and she wasn't*."

"*We women were nervous* and just kept saying it can't be true. *Finally the men came back* and told us it wasn't real."

Sometimes a person may be uncertain of his particular status in a social situation or may have to play what he regards as an unintelligent rôle because of the pressure of social customs. A man at home with his family knows what things he is supposed to do and generally enjoys freedom of action. But when he spends an evening with a friend, his behavior may become more restricted. If there is a draft in the room, is it his business to shut the window? If he doesn't like the radio program, can he turn to another station? Some people listening to the broadcast may have had their normal activities thwarted for this reason.

"We were at a party. Everybody was frightened. *I wanted to see if other stations had the program but the others wanted to hear the end of the broadcast*."

For some people *the immediacy of the danger* was apt to be a partial determinant of their reactions. They happened to be listening in a geographical zone close to the scene of the invasion and might therefore feel more personally involved in the catastrophe.

"*When the Martians started coming north* from Trenton we got really scared. *They would soon be in our town.*"

"*I wasn't frightened until they said the gas was within a few miles of us.*"

A final possible characteristic of the listening situation was the *separation from one's usual family circle.* A person who is away from loved ones for whom he is normally responsible or upon whom he is normally dependent may in such a situation have so strong a desire to join them that any other behavior seems irrelevant.

"My wife and I and two friends from next door were listening together. I was scared, everybody in the room was scared, too. *We didn't do anything except worry— especially about our son who was in Woodbridge.* It was terrible when they mentioned Woodbridge in the broadcast. But there was nothing to do."

"My husband and I were driving in the car with some friends. It was the first time *we had left our little girl home. My first thought was to get to her fast.*"

These are some of the psychological influences that might operate in different listening situations. In examining the evidence it must be remembered that none of these influences is independent of others. Several of them may be needed to interpret any one result.

*Evidence of the effects of listening situations.* Table 11 shows that persons who were told to tune in did behave less rationally than others. This is probably due both to the original attitude the listener adopted and to the further corroborating effect of another person's judgment.

## TABLE 11

REASON FOR TUNING IN COMPARED TO SUCCESS
OF ORIENTATION

| Reasons | Successful orientation (per cent) | Unsuccessful orientation (per cent) | Total per cent | Total number |
|---|---|---|---|---|
| **Tuned to** | | | | |
| Mercury Theatre | 60 | 40 | 100 | 10 |
| Happened to listen | 49 | 51 | 100 | 53 |
| **Told to listen** | | | | |
| to news | 25 | 75 | 100 | 36 |

Persons who were in listening situations which were relatively strange to them were also less likely to check successfully and therefore more likely to become frightened (Table 12). This seems due to the anxiety created

## TABLE 12

LISTENING SITUATION COMPARED TO SUCCESS OF
ORIENTATION

| Listening situation | Successful orientation (per cent) | Unsuccessful orientation (per cent) | Total per cent | Total number |
|---|---|---|---|---|
| Usual family present | 48 | 52 | 100 | 50 |
| Part of family present | 42 | 58 | 100 | 19 |
| **No family present** | | | | |
| With friends | 16 | 84 | 100 | 19 |
| Alone[10] | 55 | 45 | 100 | 11 |

[10] The apparent success of the checking behavior of people who were alone has not been commented upon in the text since the difference between the percentages is spurious when other factors are considered. The other differences, however, are not cancelled out by other influences.

when other members of the family are absent and to the lack of any well defined rôle a person has when he is in a social situation that is either relatively unfamiliar or laden with mores he cannot break.

Eleven of the persons interviewed in detail had listened to the broadcast in some public place. It is not surprising to find that eight of these were men under forty years of age. These eleven people were carefully matched by sex, age, amount of education, and degree of fright with eleven other persons interviewed. In spite of the small numbers in these two groups, revealing differences in their behavior appear. Those who listened in public places saw more people who were frightened and their own behavior seemed to be more violent than did that of members of the control group. Especially significant is the difference in the number of people in the two groups who failed to make any checks whatever. Eight of the eleven who listened in public did not attempt to check (five of these had high school education), whereas only one person in the control group made no effort to do so. From a scrutiny of the behavior of the members in each of these groups, one is left with the impression that those who were in public were more confused and more terror-stricken because they were away from home, worried about their families, and surrounded by so many other people who were frightened. This does not mean, however, that mere numbers cause less rational behavior. The influence of a group is likely to depend more on the homogeneity of the members' purposes and interests than the actual size of the group. Furthermore, excited people have a tendency to cluster together more than those who remain calm and a group might, therefore, be a result rather than a cause of fright.

A comparison of the degree of fright and the location of the persons interviewed, suggests that the listening situation of those who were within possible range of immediate danger was different from that of persons somewhat farther removed. Since it happened that the study was conducted from Princeton, the interviews were almost all made in the northern New Jersey area for reasons of supervision, convenience and economy. Fortunately the first Martian machine landed only a few miles from the source of the investigation. Seventy per cent of the people interviewed who lived near the scene of the invasion (the vicinity of Trenton and Princeton) were frightened; 50 per cent of those in or south of Newark, and 40 per cent of those living north of Newark were frightened.

When the excitement of the people interviewed in the CBS nation-wide survey who took the program as news is related to their distance from the Martian attack, the tendency is again found for people living at a greater distance from Grovers Mill, N.J., to be less frightened. Two-thirds of the persons interviewed in this study who lived in the immediate vicinity of the invasion (New York, New Jersey, and Pennsylvania) were frightened; 60 per cent of persons not in the immediate locality but within 500 miles of it, 57 per cent of those within a 1000-mile radius and 53 per cent of those within a 2000-mile radius were frightened. The one inconsistency in the trend is that 65 per cent of the persons living more than 2000 miles away (those on the West Coast) who thought the broadcast was a news report were definitely upset. No satisfactory explanation of the Far

Western reactions is found in the data. Martian machines were, after all, reported to be falling all over the country.

When we study the characteristics of the persons for whom checks were made by other people and compare them to all the remaining persons in our sample who listened in a group and who did not have the program verified for them, it appears that they were people whose status in the group required them to play a more submissive rôle.[11] Young people, women, and uneducated people were less apt to take the initiative in checking the program themselves (Table 13). This result

## TABLE 13
### PROPORTION FOR WHOM SOMEONE ELSE CHECKED

| Age | Per cent | Number for whom others checked | Total number |
|---|---|---|---|
| 50 or over | 17 | 2 | 12 |
| 35-49 | 26 | 10 | 38 |
| 20-34 | 29 | 9 | 31 |
| Under 20 | 58 | 7 | 12 |
| *Sex* | | | |
| Men | 13 | 5 | 35 |
| Women | 29 | 23 | 58 |
| *Education* | | | |
| High school or more | 24 | 11 | 46 |
| Less than high school | 36 | 17 | 47 |

[11] The reader will recall that in constructing the original fourfold classification of listeners on the basis of the adjustment they made, 36 cases were discarded—28 because someone else checked for them, six because they accidentally discovered the program was a play, two because they were anomalous. Table 13 is based upon analysis of these 28 persons who had the program examined for them and compares them to the total number listening in a group and who had no checks made for them.

does not necessarily mean that "submissive" people were less likely to check for themselves. The submissiveness, in this instance, was due to the social context within which the individual was placed.

*Summary.* Critical ability alone is not a sure preventive of panic. It may be overpowered either by an individual's own susceptible personality or by emotions generated in him by an unusual listening situation. If critical ability is to be consistently exercised, it must be possessed by a person who is invulnerable in a crisis situation and who is impervious to extraneous circumstances.

*"Being in a Troublesome World"*

# CHAPTER VII ☼ THE HISTORICAL SETTING

THE characteristic thoughts and judgments of any group of people are deeply rooted in the culture that surrounds them. The prevailing social conditions provide the context within which the individual must develop and make his adjustment. We naturally wonder if the social setting in the United States on October 30, 1938 was particularly conducive to the panicky behavior of people who happened to hear the broadcast. Are the times more out of joint now than they were in the golden 'nineties or in 1925? Were there fewer people able to orient themselves properly in 1938 than there might have been in other historical periods had a comparable situation arisen? And if conditions were particularly disturbed, did they affect all people equally? These are essentially questions for the historian and sociologist of the future. But with our present perspective and our present evidence we can discern certain characteristics of the social background which contributed to the arousal of the panic.

## Instability of Important Social Norms

When a culture is highly stable and in a state of complete equilibrium, it means that the frames of reference of the individuals constituting the culture are in complete conformity with the norms of that culture. It means, furthermore, that the frames of reference of individuals are, for them, completely adequate pathways in an environment that is satisfying their needs. Such an ideal state of affairs has certainly never existed for long in any large cultural group. Unrest, change, frustration, dissatisfaction are the rule. For at least a segment of the population current norms are inadequate to meet personal physical and psychological needs. Individual frames of reference either do not conform to accepted norms, as is the case with the radical thinker, or do not adequately explain to the individual the dissatisfaction he is experiencing, as is the case with those who frankly confess they don't know what the remedy is, those who try one remedy after another, or those who land in the camp of a leader, such as Dr. Townsend, who has an oversimplified but understandable solution.

At the time of the Martian invasion many social norms, with their corresponding personal habits, were in a state of flux and change, many of the previously accepted social standards were either proving themselves inadequate to accommodate human needs or were in danger of being overthrown by outside ideologies. In either case many of the individuals who composed the culture were perplexed and confused.

*Unsettled Conditions.* Particularly since the depression of 1929, a number of people have begun to wonder whether or not they will ever regain any sense of economic security. The complexity of modern finance and government, the discrepancies shown in the economic and political proposals of the various "experts," the felt threats of Fascism, Communism, prolonged unemployment among millions of Americans—these together with a thousand and one other characteristics of modern living—create an environment which the average individual is completely unable to interpret. Not only do events occur that he is unable to understand, but almost all of these events seem to be completely beyond his own immediate control, even though his personal life may be drastically affected by them. He feels that he is living in a period of rapid social change, but just what direction the change should take and how it may be peacefully accomplished he does not know. For the most part, the potential consequences of forthcoming events are unpredictable.

This situation is not something known only to the public official, the big businessman, or the social scientist. The masses of people themselves know all this most poignantly. The material consequences of a disturbed economic order are not difficult for anyone to recognize. And most important for our purposes are the psychological consequences in terms of personal anxieties, ambitions, and insecurities of this awareness that all is not right with the world. A few random observations will illustrate what these unsettled conditions actually mean to people.

A recent poll of the American Institute of Public Opinion contained the question, "If you lost your present job (or business) and could not find other work, how long do you think you could hold out before you would have to apply for relief?"[1] The answers to this question reflect the basic insecurity of over half the population.[2]

[1] Release of April 2, 1939.

[2] See *Consumer Incomes in the United States*, a report of the National Resources Committee for a graphic account of income distribution in the United States during 1936. Also the National Resources Committee report, *The Structure of the American Economy*, Part I: *Basic Characteristics*, 1939. Although the report has been widely quoted, the real significance of the low standards of living prevailing in the country are difficult to appreciate in any personal context unless one can actually observe the consequences or feel their implications in such books as *Grapes of Wrath, These Are Our Lives, Middletown in Transition.*

| | |
|---|---|
| Persons on relief already | 17% |
| Could hold out one month or less | 19 |
| One to six months | 16 |
| Six months up to three years | 13 |
| Three years and over | 35 |

The same ballot asked persons what social class they felt they belonged to and of what income class they considered themselves to be members. The answers to these two questions show that whereas only 6 per cent of the population regards itself as belonging to the lower *social* class and 88 per cent believe they are in the middle class, 31 per cent regard themselves as members of the lower *economic* class. Hence for a quarter of the population there is a discrepancy between their income and the social status to which they belong.

Popular education, advertising, and mass media of communication have deluged people with a knowledge of the potential abundancies of life. They derive real needs for automobiles, central heating, indoor plumbing, and dozens of other things which are now within their range of vision. Even in our small sample of case studies, we found that when people were asked to indicate from a list of eighteen possibilities, "Which of the following would you most like to have?" (such as a pretty home, travel, professional advancement), those persons with more than high school education checked twice as many things as less educated people. If education should be further extended while economic conditions remained static, one could safely predict that the discrepancy between the aspiration levels and the achievement levels of the masses would become even greater.

In the case of certain listeners to this broadcast, the general confusion in economic, political and social conditions does seem to have been a major cause of fantastic interpretation. And it was the people who were closest to the borderline of economic disaster who were most apt to take the program as news. We have already shown the high relationship between education and economic status and have seen that people of low education oriented themselves least adequately. But even when we equate people by their educational level and then compare their adjustment to the broadcast according to their economic circumstances, we find that poorer people tended to assume a false standard of judgment more frequently than others, irrespective of education (Table 14).

TABLE 14

PROPORTION OF PEOPLE IN DIFFERENT EDUCATIONAL AND ECONOMIC GROUPS WHO INTERPRETED THE PROGRAM AS NEWS (CBS SURVEY)

| Economic Status | Education | | |
| | College (per cent) | High school (per cent) | Grammar school (per cent) |
| --- | --- | --- | --- |
| High | 28 | 31 | 43 |
| Average | 25 | 34 | 45 |
| Low | 0 | 44 | 53 |

A few comments from the case studies will show how people felt, and why they were suggestible to news which perhaps seemed little less confused than the confused world they already knew.

"Everything is so upset in the world that *anything might happen*."

"Things have happened so thick and fast since my grandfather's day that *we can't hope to know what might happen now.* I am all balled up."

"Ever since my husband lost his job a few years ago, *things seem to have gone from bad to worse.* I don't know when everything will be all right again."

*"Being we are in a troublesome world, anything is liable to happen.* We hear so much news every day—so many things we hear are unbelievable. Like all of a sudden 600 children burned to death in a school house, or a lot of people being thrown out of work. Everything seems to be a shock to me."

For many persons another bewildering characteristic of our present civilization is the mystery of science. For certain people without scientific training or without sufficient personal ability, initiative or opportunity to investigate the mechanisms surrounding them, the telephone, the airplane, poison gas, the radio, the camera are but specific manifestations of a baffling power. The principles by which such things operate are completely unknown. Such devices come from a world outside and lie within a universe of discourse completely foreign to the perplexed layman. Scientists in general are frequently referred to as "they." Many variations of this theme are found in the case studies. If science can create the things we have, why can't it create rocket ships and death rays?

*"I hear they are experimenting* with rocket ships and it seems possible that we will have them."

"So many odd things are happening in the world. *Science has progressed so far* that we don't know how far it might have gone on Mars. The way the world runs ahead anything is possible."

*War Scare.* This broadcast followed closely on the heels of a European war crisis. Not only did the crisis seem to be a very real one, but it was perhaps at the time a more widely known one than any in history— thanks to the medium of radio and the ingenuity and resourcefulness of the large broadcasting companies who had special reporters on the spot. During August, September and part of October 1938 millions of Americans were listening regularly to their radios, to the latest stories of a developing international crisis. Probably never before in the history of broadcasting had so many people in this country been glued to their sets. Stations at all hours were willing to interrupt prearranged programs for the latest news broadcast. Hence both the technique and the content of this broadcast tended to fit into the existing mental context which had resulted from world events of the previous weeks.

When our interviewers asked, "What major catastrophe could happen to the American people?" three-fourths of those in the frightened group as contrasted to half of those in the non-frightened group answered war or revolution. Evidence of the same feeling is seen in answer to the question, "What sort of a catastrophe did you think it was?" Here the largest single category of response, except that of a Martian invasion, was the belief that the catastrophe actually was an act of war or some foreign attack. Over a fourth of the people who were disturbed or frightened by the broadcast gave such answers. Further expression of the fear of war is revealed in the images that listeners had of the actual invaders. Although about half of the people who were frightened or disturbed had fantastic pictures of the invaders as Martians, giants, or creatures of semi-human form, almost one-fifth of them reported that they had visions of soldiers attacking with advanced military weapons. Persons in the frightened group were, then, apparently more concerned about war.

The European war scare left some persons bewildered and confused, with a very real, if vague dread of a new war. Others had definite ideas of the potential source of trouble, localizing it chiefly in Germany or Japan. The instability of the former peace-time norms and the fear that these would be upset in favor of new norms that were personally dangerous and unwanted was clearly reflected in the case studies.

"*The war talk has us so upset.* Conditions are so unsettled since Chamberlain went to see Hitler."

"*I feel insecure* because although we are not in the war, we are so near it. I feel that with new devices on airplanes, it is possible for foreign powers to invade us. I listened to every broadcast during the European crisis."

"*I'm afraid* of all those people in Europe, they could do anything."

"I felt the catastrophe was *an attack by the Germans,* because Hitler didn't appreciate Roosevelt's telegram."

"The announcer said a meteor had fallen from Mars and I was sure he thought that, but *in back of my head I had the idea that the meteor was just a camouflage.* It was really an airplane like a Zeppelin that looked like a meteor and *the Germans were attacking* us with gas bombs. The airplane was built to look like a meteor just to fool people."

"I felt *it might be the Japanese*—they are so crafty."

A few people interpreted the invasion as an extension of the war against the Jews.

"The Jews are being treated so terribly in some parts of the world, *I was sure something had come to destroy them* in this country."

"I worry terribly about the future of the Jews. Nothing else bothers me so much. I thought *this might be another attempt to harm them.*"

*The thrill of disaster.* It is a well known fact that people who suffer deeply or whose lot in life is generally miserable frequently compensate for their situations by seeking some temporary change or escape from their troubles. Dull lives may be cheered with bright clothing or gaudy furniture, harassed breadwinners may become fixtures at the local beer hall, worried housewives may zealously participate in religious orgies, repressed youths may identify themselves for a few hours with the great lovers or gangsters of the silver screen. There are many socially accepted ways of escape from the responsibilities, worries, and frustrations of life—the movies, the pulp magazines, fraternal organizations, and a host of other devices thrive partially because their devotees want surcease from their woes.

In addition to these more obvious escapes, there are two other conditions that may resolve the problems such persons face. In the first place, some social upheaval may dissipate the circumstances that create the frustration. The early days after a revolution generally bring with them freedom and license. Sometimes the upheaval may be of such a nature that the individual will in the end be in a worse situation than he was before. But because of the intense worries or anxieties he has, he may consciously or unconsciously welcome the cataclysm. Take, for example, a bank clerk who has embezzled certain funds to help a needy family. His conscience may bother him and he may always have the dread that some day he will be caught. But one day the bank is blown up, all the records are destroyed and he himself is badly injured. It is not hard to imagine that such a man would greet such a catastrophe. A few persons represented in the case studies showed signs of welcoming the invasion and their consequent extermination because of the relief it would give them.

"*I was looking forward with some pleasure to the destruction of the entire human race* and the end of the world. *If we have Fascist domination* of the world, *there is no purpose in living anyway.*"

"My only thought involving myself as a person in connection with it was a delight that if it spread to Stelton *I would not have to pay the butcher's bill.*"

"I looked in the icebox and saw some chicken left from Sunday dinner that I was saving for Monday night dinner. I said to my nephew, '*We may as well eat this chicken*—we won't be here in the morning.' "

"The broadcast had us all worried but I knew *it would at least scare ten years' life out of my mother-in-law.*"

Another way in which people may get relief from their troubles is by submerging their own responsibilities and worries into a battle their whole society is having with some threatening force. We know, for example, that the suicide rate decreases in war time, presumably because potential suicides gain new securities and feel new responsibilities that are socially valued. Some of the frightened persons to the broadcast had a feeling of self-importance while they were listening or relaying vital information regarding the invasion to uninformed friends whom they thought they were helping. They were temporarily a member of the "in" group.

"I urged my husband to listen and said *it was an historical moment* possibly and he would be sorry afterwards to have missed it."

"*It was the thrill of a lifetime*—to hear something like that and think it's real."

"I had never heard anything like it before and I was excited even after I knew what it was about. *I felt like telling somebody all about it.*"

Others seemed to enjoy the broadcast despite their fear because the event was aligning them with other people in a conflict for rights, privileges, or ideals they had been carrying on alone or with a minority group. A Jewish woman reported, for example:

"I realized right away that *it was something that was affecting everybody, not only the Jews,* and I felt relieved. *As long as everybody was going to die,* it was better."

Although comparatively rare, these instances of an ambivalent attitude to the ensuing destruction do serve as a mirror of the times. Such persons would probably not have experienced any pleasure or relief from their worries had they lived in a more ideal social order where democracy was secure, where every person played a rôle, or where money, food, or houses were plentiful.

So far we have indicated that the broadcast would not have aroused an extensive panic if people had enjoyed greater educational advantages which they might have followed through with satisfying jobs, sufficiently rewarding to accommodate more of their needs. The times also seemed out of joint because of the threat of an impending war in which this country might become involved. These dislocations in the culture probably account in large measure for the emotional insecurity we have found so important and for the lack of critical ability discovered especially in the lower education and income brackets of the population.

Throughout the whole discussion so far we have stressed the personal and unique nature of the subjective context which the listener called upon to interpret the broadcast. In our analyses we have been forced to conceptualize these various contexts by using classificatory rubrics. But as the author of the *War of the Worlds* has pointed out, "the forceps of our minds are clumsy forceps and crush the truth a little in taking hold of it."[3] Before seeking any final generalizations with which to explain the nature of a panic, we shall turn therefore to case studies of a few individuals who were panic-stricken to see how the factors we have mentioned so far are in individual lives interwoven with individual listening experiences.

[3] H. G. Wells, *Experiment in Autobiography*, New York: Macmillan, 1934, p. 180.

# " My Background "

# CHAPTER VIII ✡ THE INDIVIDUAL CASE

IN the preceding chapters we have studied the probable causal influence of many different factors. We have discussed the importance of critical ability, of personality characteristics influencing susceptibility to panic behavior, of the listening situation, and of the cultural context in which the broadcast occurred. We have never meant to imply that these different factors act independently. Only for methodological reasons must they be studied separately. We can carry our story one step nearer to completion if we see how these various influences are patterned in individual cases.

Unfortunately it would be impracticable to present here the 135 case studies available from the interviews. Each gives a fascinating story in itself; if each were studied a fuller appreciation of the intricacy of the panic would result. We shall content ourselves with a few examples. These are not meant to be life-histories in any complete sense: they are merely relevant threads of the personal story as gathered in an interview lasting approximately an hour.[1] The interview schedule was compiled to obtain certain standardized information but it was flexible enough to allow for expressions of individual habits, values, maladjustments and the like.

Six sample stories are given below: two well educated people, two economically insecure people, and two religious people. In each pair, one person was frightened, one person was not. This selection was made to show

[1] The interview schedule will be found in Appendix B. For a discussion of the case study as a method for psychological research, see Gordon Allport, *Personality*, New York: Holt, 1938, pp. 389-99.

that there are enormous individual differences within each of these categories.

### Well Educated—Frightened

Mr. Robbins is twenty years old, single, a junior in a New Jersey college. His father is an executive in a large business concern. The family is very well to do. Mr. Robbins, Jr., has his own car and his own stocks. He is a Protestant and occasionally attends church.

Young Robbins was driving in his car with a friend. They were returning to college after visiting the friend's girl. They were just ready to cross the New Jersey border when they tuned in to station WABC. There was dance music and then a news flash telling of the meteor. Robbins was admiring the Columbia broadcasting news reports for they seemed to have people on the spot for all emergencies. When Professor Pierson from Princeton began to talk, Robbins thought he had heard of him and soon began to get worried. He and his friend were very upset when they learned that the route to Trenton was closed. Since his family lived in New Jersey, he stopped at a drugstore to phone and see if they were all right. There were four people in the drugstore and he excitedly told them the news. In the phone booth he was told that the lines were jammed and he couldn't get the call through. By the time he got out of the phone booth, the people in the drugstore were hysterically listening to the radio. He became convinced that "something was wrong" and decided to drive back to rescue his friend's girl. While driving at top speed they kept the radio tuned and heard the Secretary of the Interior which meant to them that "control was out of our hands." He turned the radio off because he "could not bear to hear the worst." He prayed "if there is a God to help us now." "I was waiting for doom to strike. I could practically smell the gas." They tuned to some other stations shortly to get other reports. Then they tuned back to WABC to hear the announcer say his was the last station on earth. Then they knew it was a play. But they were drenched in perspiration. Robbins could not digest his food properly for the next few days and said he lost five pounds during the evening.

Robbins's answers in the interview indicate that in spite of a good deal of formal training, he is a man of conventional tastes and average intelligence. When asked what magazines he read he indicated *Esquire, Readers' Digest, Colliers*. He said he read no books other than those assigned to him. In the newspapers he is chiefly interested in sports, society, and foreign news. When asked about his interests he mentioned tennis and the advertising business. This conformity to the social group seems due not merely to Robbins's age. In answer to the question concerning the things he was most proud of he said, "My background, my family tree, and my advanced knowledge."

This man probably knows more than the average person but he lacks the ability to think independently. Hence he is particularly susceptible to prestige suggestion. He was inclined to believe the broadcast because it came over CBS which had a "good reputation for news." The Princeton professor and the government official greatly impressed him. His knowledge and education are for him a matter of social standing rather than sources upon which he can draw for understanding. He prays to "God if there is one" rather than trust his knowledge. All his knowledge did for him was to make him realize that "every phenomenon is possible." This means that for a person as conventional as he is, every danger will be regarded as real if it is presented with authority.

Very important in accounting for Robbins's reaction is the fear he has that something will happen to make him financially insecure. He pictures as the major catastrophe that could occur in the United States "a great class struggle in the not distant future. Unless the quality of the people running the country improves the country will degenerate." "Things are very insecure at present. The President is meddling into everything and as long as he is in power things cannot improve." In the war crisis during the fall of 1938 he was not concerned about the people involved but about "business and my own stocks." Here was a crisis that was affecting him drastically, together with his friends and his family. These were precisely the people he had always feared were scheduled for trouble and his deep worry for his class gave him a standard of judgment which made him believe that "the end of our civilization" (but not the end of the world) had come.

## Well Educated—Not Frightened

Dr. Hamilton is a physician, twenty-nine years old, married with one small child. At present he is just building up his own private practice in a New Jersey industrial town. He has saved enough money during his last two years' work as doctor in a CCC camp to pull him through the uncertain year ahead of him. He is a Protestant but never goes to church. He lives in a rented house with his office downstairs and living quarters upstairs. He has his own car and telephone.

Dr. Hamilton was listening to the radio in his office around 7:50. Then he was interrupted and came back when the *War of the Worlds* broadcast was on "when they got the artillery out." He had missed the first part and did not know the program was a play. For a moment he believed the reports but quickly doubted the reality of the stories because of the rapidity with which things moved. He tuned to a couple of other stations and then turned back to Welles and enjoyed the play. He thinks the idea of Martians "is fun to play with but there is not much to back it up."

For Dr. Hamilton life is interesting and satisfactory. When asked what things in his life he would want to have different, he answered, "Not a thing at the moment. Of course, I would like to have a better established practice." There is no doubt in his mind, however, that he will soon be able to achieve the latter. He says that he worries less than other people and thinks he has "always had things pretty lucky."

The doctor's wishes are free of any desire for self-aggrandizement. No items of social standing are checked. They are devoid of any hint of a feeling of personal insufficiency or incompleteness. He feels neither threatened from within nor from without. This is not because he is ignorant of possible misfortunes for he reads a great many books on economics, science, politics, philosophy and biography. He seldom reads magazines. The only worry he has is that we might be involved in a war in which he would be drafted. This might mean the destruction of his work and he himself might be crippled. The only thing he is afraid of is that he "would lose the use of his hands." He is not afraid of anything except physical impacts which he cannot control. And war, with all its destructiveness, he regards contemptuously as the result of other people's foolishness.

Dr. Hamilton is a person of more than average analytical ability. He is free of sentimentality and impatient with people who live "humdrum existences." He says he is not proud of anything—only content. He does "not play around with ideas" unless there is some data to base them on.

It is clear from these two case studies that "education" alone is no sure insulation from panic. The personalities of Robbins and Dr. Hamilton are very different. Each has used formal training for different purposes. For Robbins, knowledge produces a passive concern with events; for Hamilton, it is a tool which he uses to obtain the adjustment he wants. For Robbins, life is a matter of carrying on a tradition which he believes is now seriously threatened; for Hamilton, it is something he feels he has mastered and to which he looks forward with confidence.

### Economically Insecure—Frightened

Mr. Lewis is a young man, twenty-four years of age, employed testing calibrators. He is single and lives with his ailing mother who is completely dependent on him. They own a home in a working-class neighborhood in a New Jersey city, have no phone but a '36 model car. He has a Catholic background but never goes to church. Having finished high school he is now studying to become a fashion designer.

He was visiting at a friend's home when the friend suddenly called him into the room where he was listening to the radio telling him that "we are being invaded." He first thought it was all "baloney," but upon hearing the gunfire at familiar places and when his friend was so utterly convinced that the whole broadcast was true he, too, accepted it as such. They both got in the car to warn his family and the neighbors. On the ride he smelled the gas the announcer had been talking about and also saw red in the sky. His only concern was "to flee the city." They listened to the radio only for a short while. Everybody in his friend's house was rushing away. He thought the announcer was talking about a gas that would destroy the eastern part of the country. For him it was a temporary catastrophe. The army would rush to the people's aid. When home he turned the radio on—the announcer was just telling that the "gases had passed over." Incidentally he looked at the radio page and saw the announcement of a play. So he went up to the newspaper office to discover that "other people had made fools of themselves too."

His main objection to the broadcast is "not the dramatic content but the use of actual names." He admits himself that the thing that made him inclined to believe in the broadcast was "the proximity to the place where I live." The general "hysteria" of the people he was with also affected him. He felt "we were caught right on the porch." His main concern was: "Now I will not be able to finish school. Next I thought about my family—my mother, sitting unaware of the catastrophe."

Mr. Lewis's reaction is not founded on a lack of intellectual ability to approach the situation described in the broadcast. Although without a great amount of education he is intelligent and interested in understanding things clearly. He reads four newspapers daily, two of them, *The New York Post* and *The Daily Worker*, very carefully. He mentions as his most absorbing interests literature and economics. He reads *The Nation* and *The New Masses* regularly as a subscriber. He finds no time now to read books because he is working very hard. But he excuses it by saying "he used to before." His favorite radio programs are "symphonic broadcasts, F. D. R. speeches." He has followed the Czechoslovakian crisis closely, "always waiting to hear the worst." As the most useful developments in the last twenty years he considers "machinery," most dangerous he considers "Fascism." Rocket ships and interplanetary communication he considers "slightly possible in future times." He feels that "man controls events on this earth." When asked if life is possible on Mars he answered "Why not? Of course I have read that life there is possible only under very difficult conditions but still there might be other forms of life than our own." He is not a scholar but he is an alert sort of person trying to educate himself on the track of things. The best indication of his intellectual clear mindedness is the fact that despite his fear of Fascism, and his belief in some sort of life on Mars, he did not interpret the broadcast as either an invasion of the Nazis or the Martians. He believed it to be a "temporary catastrophe" which involved personal danger and an individual end of him, his friends and neighbors. It meant to him "not being able to finish school," that is, not being able to get to a stage where he could do the kind of work he wanted. It also meant to him "having my mother sit there unaware of the catastrophe," that is, not being able to take care of her. In brief, the broadcast meant to him the failure of his personal life. He accepted it as the interruption of his life rather than as a catastrophe related to some meaningful concept. The broadcast was accepted as true not because the "invasion from Mars" made any sense to him, not because the "end of the world" was a familiar frame of reference, but because he knew no reason why anything bad should not happen to him.

All the answers given to questions concerning his personal life point to great insecurity. This insecurity is partly economic, inasmuch as his mother is dependent on him. But, on a deeper level it is an insecurity concerning himself and his ability to do the kind of work he would like to do. His present job consists of routine, but not secure, work which he hates but must keep to make a living. He wants to become a fashion designer. Aside from the insecurity of his present job he is questioning his abilities to be a good designer. When asked what were the things in his life which he would like to have different he answered: "A different job." When asked what he would most like to have he said: "Old-age security, job security, interesting type of work." All answers point to dissatisfaction with his present situation and his insecurity concerning the future. But when asked what were the three things he was most proud of, he did not mention his artistic talents. Instead he said: "My sincerity, and I am proud of America." In other words, there was not only no actual achievement he could point to but also no ability which might eventually provide for the desired achievement.

We cannot say whether or not Mr. Lewis is talented or whether he will ever be able to make any commercial use of latent talents. Hence it is impossible to estimate the real basis for his feeling of insecurity. But most important here is the fact that he is working against time. When asked what were the three things he was most afraid of, he said, "fear that I won't become a good fashion designer, fear that I won't live long enough to do what I want to." Since he has to work for a living, since he has not accomplished anything to date as an artist, he is chiefly concerned with what he can do with the time he has left. After all, he is only twenty-four years old and has life ahead of him. But the catastrophe told by the broadcast would have cut out precisely all his expectations. The broadcast seemed plausible to him because of its local character, and because of the fact that it was just the piece of bad luck he has been fearing would happen to him. He can fight against economic troubles and cope with spiritual demons. But he needs to be alive to do it.

His acceptance of the broadcast as true might also be due partially to a sense of relief. He has his doubts about his ability. He has set himself a task he is sincerely determined to carry out. But his aspiration is proving a burden. He admits that "life often seems futile." This "temporary catastrophe" would free him from his present responsibilities to himself and to others.

### Economically Insecure—Not Frightened

Mr. Chandler is thirty-six years old, married with no children. He is a painter but has been out of work most of the time ever since the depression. He lives in an apartment in a poor semi-business section of a New York suburb. He has no car or telephone. He finished grammar school and then went to business school. He is a Protestant and goes to church occasionally.

Mr. Chandler tuned to the Orson Welles broadcast incidentally. His wife and her sister's family were with him. He started to listen "when a meteor had fallen." "When I heard that I was very much interested. I have always been interested in things of that kind. I thought maybe my brother-in-law could drive me to the place where the meteor had fallen. I listened further. But when the reporter said he and a professor had travelled eleven miles in ten minutes it seemed impossible. As a result of the news flashes the streets would be crowded. They could not possibly have gotten there so fast. So I took up a newspaper and saw it was a play. From then on it was so fantastic I would not have believed it anyway."

Mr. Chandler accepted the story first as true because of the topic and the technique used. But despite the fright of his co-listeners, he was doubtful almost immediately. He made adequate checks by consulting the paper and noticing the regular air-mail plane which he felt would not be flying if there were something really wrong. His doubt began because of the discrepancy between the expected crowding of the streets and the reported speed of the announcer.

Chandler accepted the account of a fallen meteor as a physical phenomenon in which he was interested. He did not expect any further developments of this phenomenon. His natural reaction was that he would like to go and see the meteor. He imagined that this would be the reaction of most people and hence suspected that the streets would be crowded with cars. Since he has no car, he had to wait and get more reports from the radio. These he expected. But instead, an announcer and a professor were on the spot almost at once. And in place of hearing more about a meteor he heard about something no one could identify or describe. Rather than wait for the announcer to find an adequate terminology for the event, Mr. Chandler consulted his newspaper so that he could "place" this adventure in its proper frame of reference. He had "read a lot of adventure stories like that," and from then on enjoyed the drama.

Mr. Chandler is a man who has his own opinions about things and is not easily dissuaded. When asked how he behaved when in conversation with an older person who disagreed with him, he said he maintained his views rather than seeming to give in. Mr. Chandler furthermore is not afraid of the "unbelievable" or the "unknown," but considers them things to be physically mastered. Although not well educated in the formal sense, he reads two daily papers, listens to radio news, and reads the *National Geographic*. The interview revealed no religious interpretations. The major catastrophe he can picture happening to the American people is a natural catastrophe of some kind. When asked what he would most like to have he said, "No war, no depression and an interesting type of work," adding that everything else would be taken care of if he had these three.

Mr. Chandler takes all things at their face value apparently because of his personal courage, his own feeling of personal security, and his shrewd reasoning. When asked what were the three things he was most afraid of, he said, "Nothing." This he said, in spite of the fact that he has been out of work most of the time in the last ten years and has no money at all. The lack of money worries him but does not give him any feeling of insufficiency or inferiority for he does not believe it is in any way his fault. He spends his spare time "painting works of art" and thinks he has painted "some pretty good ones." When asked what he would like to have changed, he said, "I would like to have a job that would give me enough money and leisure to afford painting on the side."

The cases of Mr. Lewis and Mr. Chandler are in striking contrast. Both would like to be doing something else than they are doing at the moment, both would like "an interesting type of work," both would like to become artists. But for Mr. Lewis a failure as an artist would mean economic failure and a confession of inability, whereas for Mr. Chandler art is merely a hobby which he would like to indulge if he had money to study it.

Chandler feels self-sufficient and psychologically secure—given a job, no depression, and no war he thinks he could adjust himself satisfactorily. Lewis, on the other hand, wants old-age and job security—a guarantee that there will be no impacts from the outside. This difference is the more interesting since it is Lewis who now has a job. Because Lewis is psychologically insecure he is terrified by the broadcast which means that he can never be a success; because Chandler is at ease with himself and his conditions, he takes the broadcast realistically.

### Religious Person—Frightened

Miss Jane Dean is an unmarried woman, fifty-seven years old. She lives with her sister in a house she owns. Her home is in a small New Jersey town. She has a modest but secure income. Miss Dean only went to grammar school. She is a Protestant who attends services frequently.

She had tuned in the radio accidentally in company with her sister, at the time when "beings came out of the meteor." She says, "Of course I did not make any attempt to check up on the broadcast. When I hear something like that I take it for granted it is true." At 8:30, when the station identification was made, she turned her radio off, assuming that "it was the end of everything." Then she sat and prayed with her sister until a friend called her on an unrelated matter, and, during the discussion, told her it was a play. She confirmed this by calling a newspaper office. At this point she reports, "I got plenty mad. I had been asking God for forgiveness of my sins so that I would not be committed to eternal purgatory. I was glad I asked forgiveness anyhow even if I did not have to."

In Miss Dean's case there was a frame of reference quite adequate to account for her fright. She "knew that the forces of God were overpowering us, and was sure "we were given punishment at last for all our evil ways." She did not doubt the broadcast for a second because her religious beliefs had made her expect a catastrophe. As she states herself, "I knew we would be punished sooner or later."

Apparently she did not listen to the end because: "I wanted to have a chance to atone for my sins. I prayed and hoped it would do me some good. It eased our hearts so we were resigned." She did not mind death but wanted to die forgiven because "it is the life after life which is important." It is "not worthwhile" to try to save this life.

Miss Dean's mental world is a narrow one whose boundaries seem largely determined by religious dogmas and from which external events in the real world are deliberately excluded. She prides herself on not reading much in the local newspaper except the church news. She does not read any magazines because she does not want to "waste her time reading trash." On the radio she listens mainly to hymns. When asked what developments in any field she considered most useful she refused the whole idea of progress by saying "none will really help us." She is completely ignorant of scientific or other achievements and furthermore refuses even to believe they are possible. For her, people live chiefly to commit sins and to be punished for doing so. The most dangerous development in the last twenty years is the "way young people behave." Her religious background made her state that the most realistic part of the broadcast was "the sheet of flame that swept over the entire country. That is just the way I pictured the end." (There was no mention of any sheet of flame in the broadcast.)

One may assume that Miss Dean is a deeply frustrated woman who has turned fanatic since her religion is the only explanation she can find for a life bare of joys. She has made a virtue of frustration. Just what personal experiences in the past have led to her condition we do not know. She mentioned "conflicts in her life," but refused to elaborate on them.

For her it is a sin to live a full life. When asked what were the things she was most proud of she answered, "Don't you know that pride cometh before a fall?" The life after this life will compensate for her troubles. She checks as the only desirable thing, "no war in the next fifty years," leaving out all items providing for the development of personality or the enrichment of social life.

Thus for Miss Dean an end of the world is not only a plausible proposition but one that she may almost want to happen. It is an event that vindicates her beliefs and gives meaning to the kind of life she has led. She and her sister are resigned and prepared for the event while other people who have freely indulged in sin must face a horrible reckoning.

### Religious Person—Not Frightened

Mrs. Walters is fifty-five years old with two grown children. Her husband is an engineer. She has had some years of high school training and is an Episcopalian who attends services frequently. She lives in comfortable circumstances in a New York suburb.

The broadcast was for her a rather far-fetched story which sounded "like an enlargement of Buck Rogers." She did not think for a moment that it was anything but a play. She did not like it particularly because it was too horrible but listened to it all because her married son, whom she was visiting at the time, tuned it in when trying to get Charley McCarthy. She listened to the broadcast quite objectively. The events described had little meaning for her outside the context of the funny papers. She seems to have had throughout the broadcast this funny-paper frame of reference.

When she was asked how she knew that such things could happen only in stories she replied, "I am not scientifically minded. All I know about Mars is what I read in comic strips. There might be people on Mars but that would not worry me—they certainly would not be able to come here—certainly not in my lifetime or my children's either." For all Mrs. Walters knows or cares, then, there might be people living on Mars. They might be a little bit less weird than Buck Rogers, they might be different altogether. The only thing that concerns her is her conviction that they would not be able to come here and put in a physical appearance.

It is significant that in the statement quoted above she added, "not in my lifetime or my children's either." She is not unaware or hostile to the idea of human progress. She thought it was "slightly possible" that we might sometime have rocket ships. She considered radio to be the most useful development in the last twenty years, while "bombs and things used in war" were the most dangerous.

Mrs. Walters is aware of the existence of machines she knows little about, she considers it possible that things might be developed which do not exist today. But she reserves knowledge of those possibilities and the contact with them to the scientists or to future generations. Her own life is filled with events of immediate concern to her. Her chief worry is that "her children might get sick." She reads *The Woman's Home Companion* and the local newspaper from cover to cover. She is most interested in church-work, family, crocheting, playing cards." She is most proud of "family and church-work." In this limited circle of her life she is efficient and secure. She was just offered the presidency in her church organization.

Invaders do not fit anywhere into the world of this American housewife. They are "beyond the reach of her imagination"—"let superstitious people worry about them." She has no use for the concept of the "end of the world." Although she believes that God controls events on this earth she believes that the end of the world will come for her when she is called "home." Other than that there will be no end.

In the cases of Miss Dean and Mrs. Walters we have two "religious" persons. Both go to church frequently, both consider church-work important, both believe the life of men is controlled by God. Nevertheless, their reactions to the broadcast were quite contrasting.

The religions of the two women are obviously of a different kind and fulfilled a different function. For Miss Dean this life is a preliminary stage for the real life to begin after death; for Mrs. Walters this life is to be lived thoroughly without too much concern about the after-life. For Miss Dean, God is bent on punishing the sins of people on this earth; for Mrs. Walters, God is controlling men's lives but He takes no intimate interest in specific individuals. For Miss Dean, God is real, something around which her life is oriented; for Mrs. Walters, God is an impersonal concept which she takes for granted. These contrasting beliefs lead to an apparent paradox in the reactions of the women: Miss Dean who does not believe there are people on Mars becomes convinced that the world is ending; Mrs. Walters thinks there might be people on Mars but is not afraid. Miss Dean's expectation of destruction makes her think that the notion of an invasion from Mars is a "mistake" by the announcer and that the thing really happening is God's punishment through fire.

It would be an error to attribute the different reactions of these women entirely to a difference in the nature of their religious conceptions. Their faiths are rather an index—and a clear one—to the different adjustments they have made within their environments. Miss Dean is frustrated, without a family of her own, without any intellectual or social interest. The fact that she has a secure income seems to add to her isolation since she is not forced to make any contact with the world to earn her living. She plays no rôle in the world and is quite willing to be separate from it. Mrs. Walters's life, on the other hand, is firmly rooted in the people and events around her. To her nothing is real that does not occur within her own *Lebensraum*. Miss Dean's religious frame of reference is consistently extended to include the invasion, Mrs. Walters's religion deals only with this life and the funny papers, rather than the Bible, provided her standard of judgment for the broadcast.

*"Jitters Have Come to Roost"*

# CHAPTER IX ☼ WHY THE PANIC?

OUR task as investigators of the Martian invasion has been essentially to discover the causal factors for panic behavior. In our interpretation we have regarded as "causal" any psychological condition in the listener or the listening situation which engendered and sustained the belief that the broadcast was news. But not all social scientists or even all psychologists would agree that the particular type of explanation we have given for the behavior is "psychological" in the best sense. Strict behaviorists will note the absence of conditioning as an explanation; psychoanalysts will charge us with a lack of depth. Our only defense can be that we feel the particular accounting relationships we have given have a greater subsumptive power in conceptualizing the rich and varied experiences we have dealt with in this very realistic phenomenon of our social life. We would further contend that our accounting relationships are applicable to a wider range of similar problems in social psychology than others we might have used. Our final aim is understanding. We must await further studies of similar events to see if our type of understanding can lead to the most reliable predictions.

The final task is to weave together the various threads of explanation we have used. We have seen that a variety of influences and conditions are related to the panic resulting from this particular broadcast. We have found no single observable variable consistently related to the reaction, although a lack of critical ability seemed particularly conducive to fear in a large proportion of the population. Personality characteristics made some people especially susceptible to belief and fright; the influence of others in the immediate environment caused a few listeners to react inappropriately. The psychological pattern revealed by these and other influences must be shown if we are to understand the situation as a whole and not have to resort exclusively to the understanding of single, isolated cases.

## Why the Suggestion Was or Was Not Believed

What is most inconceivable and therefore especially interesting psychologically is why so many people did not do something to verify the information they were receiving from their loudspeakers. The failure to do this accounts for the persistence of the fright. To understand any panic—whether the cause is a legitimate one or not—it is necessary to see precisely what happens to an individual's mental processes that prevents him from making an adequate check-up.

The persons who were frightened by the broadcast were, for this occasion at least, highly suggestible, that is, they believed what they heard without making sufficient checks to prove to themselves that the broadcast was only a story. Those who were not frightened and those who believed the broadcast for only a short time were not suggestible—they were able to display what psychologists once called a "critical faculty." The problem is, then, to determine why some people are suggestible, or to state the problem differently, why some people lack critical ability.

There are essentially four psychological conditions that create in an individual the particular state of mind we know as suggestibility. All these may be described in terms of the concept of standard of judgment.

In the first place, individuals may refer a given stimulus to a standard or to several standards of judgment which they think are relevant for interpretation. The mental context into which the stimulus enters in this case is of such a character that it is welcomed as thoroughly consistent and without contradiction. A person with standards of judgment that enable him to "place" or "give meaning to" a stimulus in an almost automatic way finds nothing incongruous about such acceptance, his standards have led him to "expect" the possibility of such an occurrence. Thus a reactionary citizen will believe almost any rumor he hears that casts aspersions at political liberals; the communist will believe nearly all stories regarding progress in the Soviet Union; ideas or occurrences which contradict a rigidly established standard of judgment will be discarded, or overlooked.

We have found that many of the persons who did not even try to check the broadcast had preëxisting mental sets that made the stimulus so understandable to them that they immediately accepted it as true. Highly religious people who believed that God willed and controlled the destinies of man were already furnished with a particular standard of judgment that would make an invasion of our planet and a destruction of its members merely an "act of God." This was particularly true if the religious frame of reference was of the eschatological variety providing the individual with definite attitudes or beliefs regarding the end of the world. Other people we found had been so influenced by the recent war scare that they believed an attack by a foreign power was imminent and an invasion—whether it was due to the Japanese, Hitler, or Martians—was not unlikely. Some persons had built up such fanciful notions of the possibilities of science that they could easily believe the powers of strange superscientists were being turned against them, perhaps merely for experimental purposes.

Whatever the cause for the genesis of the standards of judgment providing ready acceptance of the event, the fact remains that many persons already possessed a context within which they immediately placed the stimulus. None of their other existing standards of judgment was sufficiently relevant to engender disbelief. We found this to be particularly true of persons whose lack of opportunities or abilities to acquire information or training had insufficiently fortified them with pertinent standards of judgment that would make the interpretation of the broadcast as a play seem plausible. More highly educated people, we found, were better able to relate a given event to a standard of judgment they *knew* was an *appropriate* referent. In such instances, the knowledge itself was used as a standard of judgment to discount the information received in the broadcast. These listeners, then, had the ability to refer to relevant standards of judgment which they could rely on for checking purposes and therefore had no need of further orientation.

A second condition of suggestibility exists when an individual is not sure of the interpretation he should place on a given stimulus and when he lacks adequate standards of judgment to make a reliable check on his interpretation. In this situation the individual attempts to check on his information but fails for one of three reasons: (a) he may check his original information against unreliable data which may themselves be affected by the situation he is checking. We found that persons who checked unsuccessfully tended to check against information obtained from friends or neighbors. Obviously, such people were apt themselves to be tinged with doubt and hesitation which would only confirm early suspicions. (b) A person may rationalize his checking information according to the original hypothesis he is checking and which he thinks he has only tentatively accepted. Many listeners made hasty mental or behavioral checks but the false standard of judgment they had already accepted was so pervasive that their checkups were rationalized as confirmatory evidence. For example, one woman said that the announcer's charred body was found too quickly but she "figured the announcer was excited and had made a mistake." A man noticed the incredible speeds but thought "they were relaying reports or something." Others turned to different stations but thought the broadcasters were deliberately trying to calm the people. A woman looked out of her window and saw a greenish eerie light which she thought was from the Martians. (c) In contrast to those who believe almost any check they make are the people who earnestly try to verify their information but do not have sufficiently well grounded standards of judgment to determine whether or not their new sources of information are reliable.

A third and perhaps more general condition of suggestibility exists when an individual is confronted with a stimulus which he must interpret or which he would like to interpret and when *none* of his existing standards of judgment is adequate to the task. On such occasions the individual's mental context is unstructured, the stimulus does not fit any of his established categories and he seeks a standard that will suffice him. The less well structured is his mental context, the fewer meanings he is able to call forth, the less able will he be to understand the relationship between himself and the stimulus, and the greater will become his anxiety. And the more desperate his need for interpretation, the more likely will he be to accept the first interpretation given him. Many conditions existed to create in the individuals who listened to the invasion from Mars a chaotic mental universe that contained no stable standards of judgment by means of which the strange event reported could be evaluated. A lack of information and formal educational training had left many persons without any generalized standards of judgment applicable to this novel situation. And even if they did have a few such standards these were vague and tenuously held because they had not proved sufficient in the past to interpret other phenomena. This was especially true of those persons who had been most adversely affected by the conditions of the times.

The prolonged economic unrest and the consequent insecurity felt by many of the listeners was another cause for bewilderment. The depression had already lasted nearly ten years. People were still out of work. Why didn't somebody do something about it? Why didn't the experts find a solution? What was the cause of it anyway? Again, what would happen, no one could tell. Again, a mysterious invasion fitted the pattern of the mysterious events of the decade. The lack of a sophisticated, relatively stable economic or political frame of reference created in many persons a psychological disequilibrium which made them seek a standard of judgment for this particular event. It was another phenomenon in the outside world beyond their control and comprehension. Other people possessed certain economic security and social status but wondered how long this would last with "things in such a turmoil." They, too, sought a stable interpretation, one that would at least give this new occurrence meaning. The war scare had left many persons in a state of complete bewilderment. They did not know what the trouble was all about or why the United States should be so concerned. The complex ideological, class, and national antagonisms responsible for the crisis were by no means fully comprehended. The situation was painfully serious and distressingly confused. What would happen, nobody could foresee. The Martian invasion was just another event reported over the radio. It was even more personally dangerous and no more enigmatic. No existing standards were available to judge its meaning or significance. But there was quick need for judgment and it was provided by the announcers, scientists, and authorities.

Persons with higher education, on the other hand, we found had acquired more generalized standards of judgment which they could put their faith in. The result was that many of them "knew" the broadcast was a play as soon as the monsters began crawling out of the cylinder. It was too fantastic to be real as judged by their knowledge of the known world which they had always relied on. Others "knew" that the phenomenal speeds with which the announcers and soldiers moved was impossible even in this day and age. The greater the possibility of checking against a variety of reliable standards of judgment, the less suggestible will a person be. We found that some persons who in more normal circumstances might have had critical ability were so overwhelmed by their particular listening situation that their better judgment was suspended. This indicates that a highly consistent structuration of the external stimulus world may, at times, be experienced with sufficient intensity because of its personal implications to inhibit the operation of usually applicable internal structurations or standards of judgment. Other persons who may normally have exhibited critical ability were unable to do so in this situation because their own emotional insecurities and anxieties made them susceptible to suggestion when confronted with a personally dangerous circumstance. In such instances, the behavioral consequence is the same as for a person who has no standards of judgment to begin with but the psychological processes underlying the behavior are different.

A fourth condition of suggestibility results when an individual not only lacks standards of judgment by means of which he may orient himself but lacks even the realization that any interpretations are possible other than the one originally presented. He accepts as truth whatever he hears or reads without even thinking to compare it to other information. Perhaps the clearest index of critical ability is a person's readiness to reevaluate interpretations he first receives, to look for new standards of judgment and juxtapose them against others. One of the outstanding indices of suggestibility is the complete absence of the awareness that things might be otherwise than they are made out to be. This final psychological condition of suggestibility is essentially an extreme instance of the third one mentioned. But with the important difference that in this case the problem of *selecting* and *seeking* a standard of judgment never arises.

Psychologically, then, most persons who tuned in to the broadcast as a news report were unable to verify the interpretation they heard because (1) they possessed standards of judgment that adequately accounted for the events and made them consistent with latent expectancies, (2) because they did not have adequate standards of judgment to distinguish between a reliable and an unreliable source of confirmation, (3) they had no standard of judgment and felt the need of one by means of which they could interpret the reports, thus accepting the interpretations provided by the "observers" of the events and by the prestige of radio, and (4) they had no standard of judgment and unhesitatingly accepted the one provided.

## Why Such Extreme Behavior?

Granted that some people believed the broadcast to be true, why did they become so hysterical? Why did they pray, telephone relatives, drive at dangerous speeds, cry, awaken sleeping children and flee? Of all the possible modes of reaction they may have followed, why did these particular patterns emerge? The obvious answer is that this was a serious affair. As in all other panics, the individual believed his well being, his safety, or his life was at stake. The situation was a real threat to him. Just what constitutes a personal threat to an individual must be briefly examined.

When an individual believes that a situation threatens him he means that it threatens not only his physical self but all of those things and people which he somehow regards as a part of him. This Ego of an individual is essentially composed of the many social and personal values *he* has accepted.[1] *He* feels threatened if his investments are threatened, *he* feels insulted if his children or parents are insulted, *he* feels elated if his alma mater wins the sectional football cup. The particular pattern of values that have been introcepted by an individual will give him, then, a particular Ego. For some individuals this is expanded to include broad ideals and ambitions. *They* will be disturbed if a particular race is persecuted in a distant country because that persecution runs counter to their ideal of human justice and democracy, *they* will be flattered if someone admires an idea of theirs or a painting they have completed.

Different values are accepted by a person with different degrees of conviction or felt-significance. Two people may each value democracy but one may be willing to die for it while another person would do nothing more than vote in a particular way and then sacrifice the value if it meant sacrificing other values more closely involved in his Ego. The particular pattern of values that constitutes a given individual's Ego will be due to the particular norms to which he has been exposed and which his temperament and previous experience have led him to select. People living in a given culture will tend by and large to accept similar values.

These values that become a part of the Ego, together with certain basic needs, may be considered as the source of an individual's motivation. The values correspond to derived needs which are often of just as dynamic a nature as the needs for sex, food and shelter.[2] The individual strives to preserve or to achieve the values he has acquired. More broadly speaking, he tries

---

[1] M. Sherif, *Psychology of Social Norms*, New York: Harpers, 1936, Chap. IX.

[2] G. W. Allport, *Personality*, New York: Holt, 1937, Chap. VII.

to maintain or reach a status he has learned to value and he tries to express himself.

One of the most universal of all values is, of course, life itself. Almost equally ubiquitous is the value of life for one's immediate relatives. To be sure, certain cultures teach the value of sacrificing life for an ideal and all cultures instill this value in times of national crisis. But by and large most individuals through the experience of living and the context of their culture value life.

A panic occurs when some highly cherished, rather commonly accepted value is threatened and when no certain elimination of the threat is in sight. The individual feels that he will be ruined, physically, financially or socially. The invasion of the Martians was a direct threat to life, to other lives that one loved, as well as to all other cherished values. The Martians were destroying practically everything. The situation was, then, indeed a serious affair. Frustration resulted when no directed behavior seemed possible. One was faced with the alternative of resigning oneself and all of one's values to complete annihilation or of making a desperate effort to escape from the field of danger, or of appealing to some higher power or stronger person whom one vaguely thought could destroy the oncoming enemy.

If one assumed that destruction was inevitable, then certain limited behavior was possible: one could cry, make peace with one's Maker, gather one's loved ones around and perish. If one attempted escape, one could run to the house of friends, speed away in a car or train, or hide in some gas-proof, bomb-proof, out-of-the-way shelter. If one still believed that something or someone might repulse the enemy, one could appeal to God or seek protection from those who had protected one in the past. Objectively none of these modes of behavior was a direct attack on the problem at hand, nothing was done to remove the causes of the crisis. The behavior in a panic is characteristically undirected and, from the point of view of the situation at hand, functionally useless.

The desire to be near loved ones was very common. As we have already implied this behavior was due to the fact that immediate relatives have become, for most persons, a part of the Ego. One wants to help them or be helped by them. In either case, psychologically, one is doing something for oneself, one is gaining emotional security. And if the most highly prized values are to be destroyed, then the individual feels that there is no use for him to live longer since so much of him will disappear with the values that are part of him. The patriot will die rather than have his country destroyed, the martyr will be burned at the stake rather than separate himself from his ideal, the revolutionist will suffer any hardship rather than forego his dream of a new social order.

In short, the extreme behavior evoked by the broadcast was due to the enormous felt ego-involvement the situation created and to the complete inability of the individual to alleviate or control the consequences of the invasion. The coming of the Martians did not present a situation where the individual could preserve one value if he sacrificed another. It was not a matter of saving one's country by giving one's life, of helping to usher in a new religion by self-denial, of risking the thief's bullet to save the family silver. In this situation the individual stood to lose *all* his values at once. Nothing could be done to save *any* of them. Panic was inescapable. The false standard of judgment used by the individual to interpret the broadcast was not itself the motivational cause of the behavior but it was absolutely essential in arousing the needs and values which may be regarded as the sources of the actions exhibited. A false standard of judgment aroused by the broadcast and causing the individual to be disturbed had its roots in values which were a part of the Ego.

When the broadcast was over and the truth had been learned, the evidence indicates that many persons wanted to make some relatively pertinent response to the horrifying stimulus they had experienced. They had a desire for "closure." The tremendous volume of fan mail and the many telephone calls after the broadcast indicate that people were satisfying a need to relieve the strain through which they had passed. As one letter-writer said in a postscript, "this is the first fan letter I have ever written. But I felt that I just had to do something about this. So I sat down and wrote this immediately." Others talked the event over with their friends or relatives. The interest in the experience, as reflected by newspaper accounts, lasted for several days.

## Social Significance

The particular incident we have analyzed was of interest to many persons other than psychologists. Since its roots were so deeply imbedded in both culture and personality and since its fruits so clearly reflected apparent cultural maladjustments, our account would be incomplete if we did not at least speculate on the social significance of the panic. The panic was a specific ailment in the social body, one from which it rapidly recovered. The diagnosis we have so far made should be concluded with a report on this type of case in general together with suggestions as to how such panics may be prevented. The educator and the social scientist who is a citizen as well as a scholar will ask "So what?"

Observers who took the incident casually might agree with the sociologist who believed that only unintelligent people were listening to this anyway and that the chances were slight any others would be disturbed. All our evidence seems to indicate, however, that many more persons might have been panicky had they happened to listen under what we might call optimum panic-producing conditions. There seems no reason to expect that relatively poor and uneducated persons should have been tuned to this program in any significantly great proportion. There is every reason to believe that the anxiety and fear revealed by the panic were latent in the general population, not specific to the persons who happened to participate in it.

In his column on November 2, 1938, the late Heywood Broun said, "I doubt if anything of the sort would have happened four or five months ago. The course of world history has affected national psychology. Jitters have come to roost. We have just gone through a laboratory demonstration of the fact that the peace of Munich hangs heavy over our heads, like a thundercloud."[3] Our data have indicated the rôle which the war scare of the last summer and early fall of 1938 played in producing the panic. But they also show that for many persons, the fear of war played only a secondary rôle if it indeed played any rôle at all. To imply that specific events that recently occurred in Europe and were broadcast to the United States served as the chief cause of the panic

[3] *New York World-Telegram*, Nov. 2, 1938.

would be to disregard the multitude of other factors we have found so important.

That "the course of world history" has affected us is a truism. But this course of history contains more than war crises. Just what has happened is too familiar to be recited here. Probably more important than anything else, the highly disturbed economic conditions many Americans have experienced for the past decade, the consequent unemployment, the prolonged discrepancies between family incomes, the inability of both young and old to plan for the future have engendered a widespread feeling of insecurity. And persons underprivileged financially are underprivileged educationally, not to mention the many other personal consequences of a low and insecure income.

Prolonged bewilderment combined with lack of training to seek the basic causes of maladjustment are precisely the conditions most conducive to frustration and anxiety. Individuals sooner or later are likely to rebel at a situation which is far from satisfactory and which they cannot understand. They neither have the opportunity nor the training to see the complex and contradictory bases creating their maladjustments. Yet they desire an understanding and their desire increases with their perplexity. They become highly suggestible to some simple and sovereign formula provided by a demagogue. The whole tactics of Hitler show the importance he places on providing directed relief to bewildered souls. If they are not already sufficiently bewildered, bewilderment can be manufactured by sufficient propaganda.

Just as there is little possibility that people will be wholly impervious to propaganda for war or for dictatorship until the basic economic and ideological conflicts causing wars and dictatorships are removed, so it would seem that there is little reason to expect people would be wholly insulated from panic-creating situations until the basic causes for panic are removed. It is not the radio, the movies, the press or "propaganda" which, in themselves, really create wars and panics. It is the discrepancy between the whole superstructure of economic, social, and political practices and beliefs, and the basic and derived needs of individuals that creates wars, panics or mass movements of any kind. And human needs can only be curbed by the deliberate and forceful cultivation of ignorance, intolerance, and abstention. Such practices all adherents to democracy abhor.

But the latent anxieties conducive to panic may nevertheless be minimized if the critical abilities of people can be increased. Even though the rape of a Southern white woman by a Negro is still a possibility, increased education regarding the frustrations that lead to lynchings may encourage potential mob members to investigate charges more thoroughly before taking their antisocial action. Thus while objective conditions may be slow to change, there is encouragement in the fact that our subjective reactions to these conditions may be made to change somewhat more rapidly by education. And education, we discovered, was one of the greatest preventives of panic behavior. A greater critical ability would not only enable people to distinguish between reality and fiction but it would also enable them to make more appropriate adjustments if they ever were caught in a genuinely critical situation. Just as a knowledge of hygiene and the rudiments of medicine help to prevent illness, they also help to restore the individual who is actually sick.

Our study of the common man of our times has shown us that his ability to orient himself appropriately in critical situations will be increased if he can be taught to adopt an attitude of readiness to question the interpretations he hears. But when he achieves this healthy skepticism he must have sufficient and relevant knowledge to be able to evaluate different interpretations. If he is to judge these interpretations intelligently, his knowledge must be grounded in evidence or tested experience. If this skepticism and knowledge are to be spread more widely among common men, they must be provided extensive educational opportunities. And if this final critical ability is to be used more generally by common men, they must be less harassed by the emotional insecurities which stem from underprivileged environments.

# APPENDIX A ☼ MISCELLANEOUS INFORMATION

## HOW FRIGHT AFFECTED DRIVING. PREDICTIONS OF SOCIAL SCIENTISTS

In the course of the investigation, certain findings appeared that should be included here for the sake of the record. The data are not pertinent to our main story but the information they reveal should not be completely lost.

*How fright affected driving.* Nine persons interviewed were riding in automobiles when they heard the broadcast. Three of the drivers became very frightened. The following quotations show that their anxieties had so occupied their consciousness that they were completely oblivious to the external world through which they manipulated their cars. Psychologically, these cases are comparable to those frequently reported of men in battle who do not feel pain or of people who demonstrate unusual strength or speed in crucial situations.

"You know, I had one funny reaction. I made that forty miles home in an hour flat, and I've never done so well before or since. But the funny part is that *I didn't even realize I had been driving so much faster* than usual until I got home and saw the time."

"*My girl friend pointed out to me that I had passed a couple of red lights* and I answered 'What's the difference if I get a ticket, it will only be burned anyway.' "

"I made the forty-five miles in thirty-five minutes and *didn't even realize it.* I drove right through Newburgh and *never even knew I went through it.* I don't know why we weren't killed. I was going eighty miles an hour most of the way. I remember not giving a damn, as what difference did it make which way I'd get killed. On Monday after it was all over and I started to think of that ride I was more jittery than when it was happening. The speed was never under seventy. I thought I was racing against time."

A similar reaction was reported in a letter to the writer.

"I became terribly frightened and got in the car and started for the priest so I could make peace with God before dying. Then I began to think that perhaps it might have been a story, but discounted that because of the introduction as a special news broadcast. While enroute to my destination, a curve loomed up and travelling at between seventy-five and eighty miles per hour, I knew I couldn't make it though *as I recall it didn't greatly concern me either*. To die one way or another, it made no difference as death was inevitable. After turning over twice the car landed upright and I got out, looked at the car and thought that it didn't matter that it wasn't my car or that it was wrecked as the owner would have no more use for it."

*Predictions of social scientists.* Over two hundred fifty social psychologists and sociologists returned a questionnaire which asked them to indicate some of the characteristics of people who were most likely to be frightened by the broadcast. In many ways, such a questionnaire is unfair since it presupposes that a given factor will be equally important for all people. Nevertheless, the guesses of the social scientists are interesting. They thought that older people, uneducated people, women, and persons living in large cities would tend to be most upset. When asked to indicate what differences in personality traits or capacities they would expect among those who were frightened, they stressed neuroticism, instability, and suggestibility. They were also instructed to check the degree of importance which they attributed to each of several reasons listed in predisposing people to believe the broadcast was true. The reasons together with the results of this prediction are shown in the following graph. The answers were weighted by

WEIGHTED RANKS OF IMPORTANCE
ASSIGNED BY SOCIAL SCIENTISTS

9 —

8 —   Recent war scare in Europe

7 —   General intellectual immaturity
      Prestige of commentators

6 —   General emotional immaturity

5 —   Science is a mystery

4 —

3 —

2 —   Insecurity from prolonged depression
      Insecurity from natural catastrophes

1 —   Belief that world will end sometime
      Reading of Buck Rogers, etc.

0 —   Religious beliefs

multiplying the number of "very important" checks by 2, the "moderately important" by 1, the "not at all important" by zero.

The predictions do stress many factors we have found important: education, "instability," suggestibility, intellectual and emotional maturity. Our own data do not show any significant sex or age differences as such —they disappear when other variables are considered. The predictions of the social scientists seem to underestimate the importance of religious beliefs, but this term is so broad that it can have many implications some of which would have nothing to do with susceptibility to suggestion. The social scientists appeared to be quite right in stressing the effects of the war scare and the prolonged depression.

# APPENDIX B ✵ INTERVIEW SCHEDULE[1]

*QUESTIONNAIRE FOR THE*
*ORSON WELLES INTERVIEW*

Interviewer's name...........................

1. At what time of the program did you start listening?
   a. Where did you listen to the broadcast?
2. How did you happen to start listening?
   Always listen to Welles................
   Happened to tune in................
   Someone else tuned in:
       Accidentally................
       Purposely.... ............
   Entered a room where it was on................
   Was told or called to tune in................
   Other reason................
3. a. With whom did you listen?
   b. If not with the whole family, where were the other family members?
4. Did you listen to the end of the broadcast?
       Yes................       No................
5. Did you know immediately that it was a play...........
   or did you first think that it was a real news broadcast?

[1] The interviewer referred to this schedule in asking questions of the respondent. During the interview, notes were taken and transferred immediately after the interview to a mimeographed copy of the schedule. Considerable variability occurred in the order in which the questions were answered. If one question elicited a flow of discussion which covered several points, it was not interrupted because the respondent's answers were out of order. The interviewers took notes in shorthand. Once the co-operation of the respondent had been secured, the fact that the interviewer was taking notes did not seem in the least to jeopardize the frank and free description characteristically provided.

6. Do you think that such programs should be given?
   Yes................ No................
   a. Why?

## Part I. Re: those who knew that it was a play from the beginning

1. How did you happen to know that it was a play?
2. Did you doubt for any time after you had tuned in that it was a play?
   Yes................ No................
3. If doubted: At what part of the program was it?
   a. Why just then?
   b. What made you certain that it was a play after all?
4. If you doubted: What in the program made you certain that it was only a play?
   How do you know that only such things can happen in plays? (What in respondent's personality or background accounts for his attitude?)
5. Did you like the play? Yes................ No................
6. What did you like (or dislike) about it?
7. How do you account for the fact that many people became frightened and hysterical during the broadcast?

## Part II. Re: those who believed at first that it was a real news broadcast

1. For about how long did you believe that it was a news broadcast?
   All evening (longer than actual broadcast)............
   Up to the end of the broadcast............
   For quite some time during the broadcast............

Only very shortly during the broadcast............
Was at no time very definite about it............
Other reason............

2.  A.  How did you find out that it was a play?

      a.  Detailed account of respondent's reaction. (How soon did he check, at what point of program, why just then, who made the check, what sort of checks were they, what did the checks made or offered contribute to his reaction? Why did he not make any checks?)

      b.  What did you do when you thought it was true?

2.  B.  *Interviewer*—Classify at what point and why respondent started checking.

No check made because not intended information came almost immediately............

No checks made: realized almost immediately that it could only be a play............

Checks made almost immediately to find out what it was all about, accepted it to be a play ............

Believed up to "incredible" point in broadcast: then checks were made and accepted ............

Believed up to "dangerous" point in broadcast: then checks were made and accepted ............

Checking activities started immediately but respondent was reassured of news-character through abortive checks............

No checks made: just stayed and listened to end ............

No checks made: respondent got panicky and
discontinued listening............

No checks made: respondent even refused to
accept offered checks............

3. *Note to the interviewer:* According to the type to reaction as set up in 2B two different sets of questions
have to be asked in the following. The one set ap-
plies to the first three types of the above classification, that is, to those people who cannot be classified
really as having "fallen for" the program. The other
set belongs to the remaining six types of reaction,
that is, to those people who, for a longer time, believed in the news character of the broadcast.

a. To be asked if respondent falls in one of the first
three types of reaction.

1. What kind of a catastrophe did you believe it
to be?

2. What in the program made you inclined to
doubt that it was a real news broadcast?

3. Why did you feel so?

4. What was the reaction of others in company?

5. Did you continue listening after you found
out it was a play? Yes............ No............

6. If yes: Did you like the play? Yes............
No............ Why?

7. How do you account for the fact that many
people became frightened and hysterical during the broadcast?

b. To be asked if respondent falls in one of the
remaining types of reaction.

1. What sort of a catastrophe did you think it
was?

What made you feel that such a catastrophe was possible at this time?

2. How did you picture the people who were invading?
3. What made you inclined to believe in the broadcast? Spontaneous answer.

*Trace back influences from:*

Particular knowledge about Mars which could be applied to the broadcast (get general concept of Mars).

Do you think it is possible that there is some form of life on Mars comparable to ours?

Very possible............ Slightly possible............
Not at all............          No opinion............

Past occurrences (such as the war crisis, natural catastrophes).

Have you ever been in situations before where you had a similar reaction? If so, what?

Individual past experiences:

Have you been through any natural catastrophes such as floods, hurricanes, dust storms, etc.?

Has anything occurred in your life to make you feel especially anxious for any length of time (war experience of family member, prolonged illness, etc.)?

Influences immediately preceding the listening to the broadcast (any unusual strain or occurrence during the few days previous, etc.).

General attitude toward science:

Do you think it is possible that we shall sometime have rocket ships and interplanetary communication?

Very possible............Slightly possible............
Not at all............
Religious beliefs, *Weltanschauung*
Do you believe that God can and does control
events on this earth?
Yes............ No............ No opinion............
Does man's life on this earth seem to you
meaningless, temporary, futile, etc.?
Fears, prejudices, insecurities
Are there people of any particular race or
nation that you dislike very much? If so,
why?
4. What features in the broadcast did seem particularly realistic to you?
5. What was the reaction of the other people in
your company?
6. Which part of the broadcast had you most
scared? Why?
7. What was your outstanding concern about
being involved in such a catastrophe?
8. Was there anything that made you inclined to
doubt the fact that it was a real news broadcast?

*PERSONAL DATA*

Name............ ............ Residence............................
Sex............ Age............ Married............ Single............
No. of children............
Occupation (include amount of responsibility) (if
woman, get husband's occupation)............................

....................................................................

Is the security of your job (or your husband's job)
greatly dependent on business conditions or the

friendship of certain people? (Follow this up to get idea of job security)

Education: finished grammar school........ finished high school............some years of high school............some years of college............finished college............

Religion.................... Attends services:.........................
frequently........ occasionally........ never........

Race.................... National background.......................

Economic status A........ B........ C........ D........ E........

Owns home........ rents house........ lives in apartment.....

Describe type of house or apartment (section of town, furniture)

..............................................................................................

..............................................................................................

Owns car........ Make of car........ Year of car........ Has telephone........

Do you (or your husband) carry any life insurance?
Yes............ No............

What are your favorite radio programs to which you listen frequently? (list them)

..............................................................................................

..............................................................................................

Have you followed up the broadcast of the Czecho-slovakian crisis? Yes............ No............

Which of the magazines you read do you like best?........

..............................................................................................

..............................................................................................

Do you have time to read books regularly? Yes............
No............ Occasionally............

If yes, what sort of books do you read?.......................

..............................................................................................

What newspaper(s) do you read?.............................

Which section in them do you find most interesting?
   Why?
   (Get specific information if "editorials" mentioned)

......................................................................................................

......................................................................................................

How did you spend your last vacation?............................

For whom did you vote in 1936?................................

What are the things you are most interested in? Why?

......................................................................................................

......................................................................................................

What developments (in any field) in the last twenty
   years do you consider:
                     Most useful...............................................
                     Most dangerous.........................................

What are the things in your life which you would like
   to have different?..........................................................

......................................................................................................

What are the three things you are most afraid of?.........

......................................................................................................

What major catastrophe do you picture as possible to
   the American people?...................................................

......................................................................................................

What are the three things you are most proud of?.........

......................................................................................................

Have you ever had to manage a complicated situation?
                     Yes............   No............

If yes, what situation?................................................

......................................................................................................

Which of the following would you most like to have?
                  (allow for three checks)
   Old-age security........
   High salary........
   College education for your children........
   Job security........

Safety of investments........
No war in the next fifty years........
No depression in the next fifty years........
Getting ahead in your profession........
Having some good friends........
Having a standing in the community........
Extensive travelling........
Having an interesting type of work........
Having a pretty home in a good neighborhood........
Having more variety in living........
Having a pleasant family........
No major political changes in the next decades........
Having more leisure........
Why have you checked these particular things?

Do you consider that you worry more than other people?
                    More........ Same........ Less........
What are the things you worry most about?

Has it always been so? Yes........ No........ If no, since
    when............................................................................
    ..............................................................................

If *man* ask:
    Have you within the past five years been recognized
    as the leader of any groups? More than six........ One
    to six........ None........
    In conversing with a person older than yourself whom
    you respect, on an issue about which you disagree, do
    you characteristically:
    Maintain your views in argument........
    Conciliate your opponent by seeming to agree with
    him, and yet try indirectly to carry your point........

Agree with him, at least verbally, and let it go at that........

If *woman* ask:

Have you been the recognized leader of an organized group of girls or women: More than six times........ Less than six times but more than once........ Only once........ Never....... .

Suppose a speaker asks anyone in the audience, say of fifty people, to volunteer an idea to start discussion. You have what appears to be a good idea. Do you speak out?

Usually ....... Occasionally........ Rarely........ Never........

Interviewer's impression of respondent's leadership qualities.

If respondent has stated that it is *very probable* that there is life on Mars, tell him that most scientists think it very unlikely. Get reaction.

If respondent has stated that it is *scarcely* or *not at all probable* that there is life on Mars, tell him that some eminent astronomers believe that there is. Get reaction.

Interviewer's general impression as to the respondent's personality and psychological world. (Stress on analytical abilities, economic insecurity, psychological insecurity, gullibility, specific individual characteristics, leadership)

# APPENDIX C ☼ TABLES

## TABLE 15

### PROPORTION KNOWING BROADCAST TO BE A PLAY IN DIFFERENT AGE AND EDUCATION GROUPS
#### (CBS SURVEY)

| EDUCATION | AGE | |
|---|---|---|
| | 40 *and Over* | *Under* 40 |
| High school or more | 69 | 60 |
| Less than high school | 55 | 50 |

## TABLE 16

### PROPORTION OF PEOPLE WHO APPROVE OF ROOSEVELT'S POLICIES BY EDUCATION AND ECONOMIC STATUS
#### (ANALYSIS OF AMERICAN INSTITUTE OF PUBLIC OPINION DATA. SURVEY MADE MARCH 1939)

| EDUCATION | ECONOMIC STATUS | | |
|---|---|---|---|
| | *High* (per cent) | *Average* (per cent) | *Low* (per cent) |
| College | 30 | 48 | 58 |
| High school | 42 | 55 | 63 |
| Grammar school | 42 | 53 | 65 |
| Did not finish grammar school | 26 | 63 | 70 |

## TABLE 17

### DIFFERENCES IN SUSCEPTIBILITY OF BEHAVIOR GROUPS IN DIFFERENT EDUCATIONAL LEVELS
#### (NUMBER OF POSITIVE INDICATIONS OF SUSCEPTIBILITY)

| EDUCATION | SUCCESSFUL ORIENTATION | | UNSUCCESSFUL ORIENTATION | |
|---|---|---|---|---|
| | *Number of Plus Signs* | *Total Number of Signs* | *Number of Plus Signs* | *Total Number of Signs* |
| High school or more | 32 | 152 | 59 | 165 |
| Less than high school | 18 | 75 | 70 | 172 |

# TABLE 18

## RELATION OF SUSCEPTIBILITY INDEX TO BEHAVIOR GROUPS ON DIFFERENT EDUCATIONAL LEVELS[1]

| SUSCEPTIBILITY INDEX | HIGH SCHOOL OR MORE | | LESS THAN HIGH SCHOOL | |
|---|---|---|---|---|
| | *Successful Orientation* | *Unsuccessful Orientation* | *Successful Orientation* | *Unsuccessful Orientation* |
| Susceptible* | 5 | 14 | 3 | 14 |
| Equivocal† | 4 | 3 | 1 | 4 |
| Unsusceptible‡ | 19 | 11 | 9 | 12 |
| Total persons | 28 | 28 | 13 | 30 |

[1] In Table 10 the different groups were characterized by the proportion of plus signs recorded. A susceptibility index for each individual may also be obtained by classifying each respondent according to the excess of plus signs or minus signs he receives in the seven components of the susceptibility index. Although there were seven aspects in which each case was classified, sometimes the necessary information on one of them was lacking. As a result a few individuals had an equal number of plus and minus signs and must therefore be classified mid-way between the susceptible and unsusceptible people. In spite of the fact that the 99 cases are here broken down into twelve groups, the result is still statistically significant.

* Individuals who gave more positive indications of susceptibility than negative (more plus signs than minus signs).

† Individuals in whom the number of plus and minus signs of susceptibility were equal.

‡ Individuals who had more minus signs of susceptibility than plus signs.

# INDEX

age and listening, 57
age and economic status, 148
Allport, G. W., 129, 133, 136, 167, 198
American Institute of Public Opinion, 55-8, 77, 114, 155*f.*, 223
announcements, 43*f.*
audience, regional differences in, 57
audience, size of, 55*f.*

behavior and feeling, 105-7
Benson, E., 55
Benson, L., 55
Broun, H., 202

Cantril, H., 55, 136
case study as method, 164, 167
Charlie McCarthy program, 82*f.*
checks, accidental, 102; made by others, 101*f.*; types of, 88-100; and education, 118; and reliability, 119
church attendance, 134
closure, desire for, 201
contagion of fear, 140*f.*, 146*f.*
critical ability, and education, 112-24; definition of, 111*f.*; nature of, 115-19; not sufficient preventive, 127*f.*, 138*f.*, 149

Dashiell, J. F., 142
deviate cases, 119-24
disturbing effect of other people, 142*f.*

economic insecurity, 155-8; and suggestibility, 194*f.*, 203
economic status, and education, 113*f.*, 157*f.*; and extent of listening, 57; and interpretation, 113-15; as index, 113*f.*, 113n.
education, and age, 113; and critical ability, 112-24; and increased wants, 156*f.*; and orientation, 112-24; and status, 148; and suggestibility, 192-6; as preven-

tive, 204*f.*; as substitute index, 112, 122
ego, nature of, 197*f.*
emotional insecurity, 138*f.*, 163*f.*
exceptional cases, 100-2

fantastic literature, 90, 121
fatalism, 133
Federal Communications Commission, 3, 61
*Fortune* poll, 69
fright, and checking behavior, 96; and distance from scene, 147*f.*; and driving, 207*f.*; classification by, 105*f.*; number of persons, 57*f.*; sectional differences of, 59

Gallup, G., 55

Hooper, C. E., Inc., 56, 82, 84

intelligence test, 128n.
interview schedule, 213-22

Katz, D., 55
Koch, H., 3

Lazarsfeld, P., 69, 81, 114, 131
listeners, classification of, 87-102
listening situation, 139-49; and orientation, 145*f.*; characteristics of, 140-4

mail volume, 60*f.*
Mercury Theatre, 3, 61*f.*

National Resources Committee, 155
newspaper clippings, 61*f.*
norms, instability of, 153*f.*

Odbert, H. S., 129
orientation, and checking behavior, 89-100, 116*f.*; and education, 112-24; and reasons for listening, 144*f.*

70 71 72 73   12 11 10 9 8 7 6 5 4

# harper ✦ torchbooks

## American Studies: General

HENRY ADAMS Degradation of the Democratic Dogma. ‡ *Introduction by Charles Hirschfeld.* TB/1450

LOUIS D. BRANDEIS: Other People's Money, *and How the Bankers Use It. Ed. with Intro, by Richard M. Abrams* TB/3081

HENRY STEELE COMMAGER, Ed.: The Struggle for Racial Equality TB/1300

CARL N. DEGLER: Out of Our Past: *The Forces that Shaped Modern America* CN/2

CARL N. DEGLER, Ed.: Pivotal Interpretations of American History
Vol. I TB/1240; Vol. II TB/1241

A. S. EISENSTADT, Ed.: The Craft of American History: *Selected Essays*
Vol. I TB/1255; Vol. II TB/1256

LAWRENCE H. FUCHS, Ed.: American Ethnic Politics TB/1368

MARCUS LEE HANSEN: The Atlantic Migration: 1607-1860. *Edited by Arthur M. Schlesinger. Introduction by Oscar Handlin* TB/1052

MARCUS LEE HANSEN: The Immigrant in American History. *Edited with a Foreword by Arthur M. Schlesinger* TB/1120

ROBERT L. HEILBRONER: The Limits of American Capitalism TB/1305

JOHN HIGHAM, Ed.: The Reconstruction of American History TB/1068

ROBERT H. JACKSON: The Supreme Court in the American System of Government TB/1106

JOHN F. KENNEDY: A Nation of Immigrants. *Illus. Revised and Enlarged. Introduction by Robert F. Kennedy* TB/1118

LEONARD W. LEVY, Ed.: American Constitutional Law: *Historical Essays* TB/1285

LEONARD W. LEVY, Ed.: Judicial Review and the Supreme Court TB/1296

LEONARD W. LEVY: The Law of the Commonwealth and Chief Justice Shaw: *The Evolution of American Law, 1830-1860* TB/1309

GORDON K. LEWIS: Puerto Rico: *Freedom and Power in the Caribbean. Abridged edition* TB/1371

HENRY F. MAY: Protestant Churches and Industrial America TB/1334

RICHARD B. MORRIS: Fair Trial: *Fourteen Who Stood Accused, from Anne Hutchinson to Alger Hiss* TB/1335

GUNNAR MYRDAL: An American Dilemma: *The Negro Problem and Modern Democracy. Introduction by the Author.*
Vol. I TB/1443; Vol. II TB/1444

GILBERT OSOFSKY, Ed.: The Burden of Race: *A Documentary History of Negro-White Relations in America* TB/1405

CONYERS READ, Ed.: The Constitution Reconsidered. *Revised Edition. Preface by Richard B. Morris* TB/1384

ARNOLD ROSE: The Negro in America: *The Condensed Version of Gunnar Myrdal's* An American Dilemma. *Second Edition* TB/3048

JOHN E. SMITH: Themes in American Philosophy: *Purpose, Experience and Community* TB/1466

WILLIAM R. TAYLOR: Cavalier and Yankee: *The Old South and American National Character* TB/1474

## American Studies: Colonial

BERNARD BAILYN: The New England Merchants in the Seventeenth Century TB/1149

ROBERT E. BROWN: Middle-Class Democracy and Revolution in Massachusetts, 1691-1780. *New Introduction by Author* TB/1413

JOSEPH CHARLES: The Origins of the American Party System TB/1049

HENRY STEELE COMMAGER & ELMO GIORDANETTI, Eds.: Was America a Mistake? *An Eighteenth Century Controversy* TB/1329

WESLEY FRANK CRAVEN: The Colonies in Transition: 1660-1712† TB/3084

CHARLES GIBSON: Spain in America † TB/3077

CHARLES GIBSON, Ed.: The Spanish Tradition in America + HR/1351

LAWRENCE HENRY GIPSON: The Coming of the Revolution: 1763-1775. † *Illus.* TB/3007

JACK P. GREENE, Ed.: Great Britain and the American Colonies: 1606-1763. + *Introduction by the Author* HR/1477

AUBREY C. LAND, Ed.: Bases of the Plantation Society + HR/1429

JOHN LANKFORD, Ed.: Captain John Smith's America: *Selections from his Writings* ‡ TB/3078

LEONARD W. LEVY: Freedom of Speech and Press in Early American History: *Legacy of Suppression* TB/1109

---

† The New American Nation Series, edited by Henry Steele Commager and Richard B. Morris.
‡ American Perspectives series, edited by Bernard Wishy and William E. Leuchtenburg.
*a* History of Europe series, edited by J. H. Plumb.
§ The Library of Religion and Culture, edited by Benjamin Nelson.
‖ Researches in the Social, Cultural, and Behavioral Sciences, edited by Benjamin Nelson.
° Harper Modern Science Series, edited by James A. Newman.
° Not for sale in Canada.
+ Documentary History of the United States series, edited by Richard B. Morris.
# Documentary History of Western Civilization series, edited by Eugene C. Black and Leonard W. Levy.
Λ The Economic History of the United States series, edited by Henry David et al.
¶ European Perspectives series, edited by Eugene C. Black.
** Contemporary Essays series, edited by Leonard W. Levy.
* The Stratum Series, edited by John Hale.

2

ARNOLD M. PAUL: Conservative Crisis and the Rule of Law: *Attitudes of Bar and Bench, 1887-1895. New Introduction by Author*  TB/1415

JAMES S. PIKE: The Prostrate State: *South Carolina under Negro Government.* ‡ *Intro. by Robert F. Durden*  TB/3085

WHITELAW REID: After the War: *A Tour of the Southern States, 1865-1866.* ‡ *Edited by C. Vann Woodward*  TB/3066

FRED A. SHANNON: The Farmer's Last Frontier: ....*Agriculture, 1860-1897*  TB/1348

VERNON LANE WHARTON: The Negro in Mississippi, 1865-1890  TB/1178

## American Studies: The Twentieth Century

RICHARD M. ABRAMS, Ed.: The Issues of the Populist and Progressive Eras, 1892-1912 +  HR/1428

RAY STANNARD BAKER: Following the Color Line: *American Negro Citizenship in Progressive Era.* ‡ *Edited by Dewey W. Grantham, Jr. Illus.*  TB/3053

RANDOLPH S. BOURNE: War and the Intellectuals: *Collected Essays, 1915-1919.* ‡ *Edited by Carl Resek*  TB/3043

A. RUSSELL BUCHANAN: The United States and World War II. † *Illus.*
Vol. I TB/3044; Vol. II TB/3045

THOMAS C. COCHRAN: The American Business System: *A Historical Perspective, 1900-1955*  TB/1080

FOSTER RHEA DULLES: America's Rise to World Power: 1898-1954. † *Illus.*  TB/3021

JEAN-BAPTISTE DUROSELLE: From Wilson to Roosevelt: *Foreign Policy of the United States, 1913-1945. Trans. by Nancy Lyman Roelker*  TB/1370

HAROLD U. FAULKNER: The Decline of Laissez Faire, 1897-1917  TB/1397

JOHN D. HICKS: Republican Ascendancy: 1921-1933. † *Illus.*  TB/3041

ROBERT HUNTER: Poverty: *Social Conscience in the Progressive Era.* ‡ *Edited by Peter d'A. Jones*  TB/3065

WILLIAM E. LEUCHTENBURG: Franklin D. Roosevelt and the New Deal: 1932-1940. † *Illus.*  TB/3025

WILLIAM E. LEUCHTENBURG, Ed.: The New Deal: *A Documentary History* +  HR/1354

ARTHUR S. LINK: Woodrow Wilson and the Progressive Era: 1910-1917. † *Illus.* TB/3023

BROADUS MITCHELL: Depression Decade: *From New Era through New Deal, 1929-1941* ∧  TB/1439

GEORGE E. MOWRY: The Era of Theodore Roosevelt and the Birth of Modern America: 1900-1912. † *Illus.*  TB/3022

WILLIAM PRESTON, JR.: Aliens and Dissenters: *Federal Suppression of Radicals, 1903-1933*  TB/1287

WALTER RAUSCHENBUSCH: Christianity and the Social Crisis. ‡ *Edited by Robert D. Cross*  TB/3059

GEORGE SOULE: Prosperity Decade: *From War to Depression, 1917-1929* ∧  TB/1349

GEORGE B. TINDALL, Ed.: A Populist Reader: *Selections from the Works of American Populist Leaders*  TB/3069

TWELVE SOUTHERNERS: I'll Take My Stand: *The South and the Agrarian Tradition. Intro. by Louis D. Rubin, Jr.; Biographical Essays by Virginia Rock*  TB/1072

## Art, Art History, Aesthetics

CREIGHTON GILBERT, Ed.: Renaissance Art ** *Illus.*  TB/1465

EMILE MALE: The Gothic Image: *Religious Art in France of the Thirteenth Century.* § 190 illus.  TB/344

MILLARD MEISS: Painting in Florence and Siena After the Black Death: *The Arts, Religion and Society in the Mid-Fourteenth Century. 169 illus.*  TB/1148

ERWIN PANOFSKY: Renaissance and Renascences in Western Art. *Illus.*  TB/1447

ERWIN PANOFSKY: Studies in Iconology: *Humanistic Themes in the Art of the Renaissance. 180 illus.*  TB/1077

JEAN SEZNEC: The Survival of the Pagan Gods: *The Mythological Tradition and Its Place in Renaissance Humanism and Art. 108 illus.*  TB/2004

OTTO VON SIMSON: The Gothic Cathedral: *Origins of Gothic Architecture and the Medieval Concept of Order. 58 illus.*  TB/2018

HEINRICH ZIMMER: Myths and Symbols in Indian Art and Civilization. *70 illus.*  TB/2005

## Asian Studies

WOLFGANG FRANKE: China and the West: *The Cultural Encounter, 13th to 20th Centuries. Trans. by R. A. Wilson*  TB/1326

L. CARRINGTON GOODRICH: A Short History of the Chinese People. *Illus.*  TB/3015

DAN N. JACOBS, Ed.: The New Communist Manifesto and Related Documents. *3rd revised edn.*  TB/1078

DAN N. JACOBS & HANS H. BAERWALD, Eds.: Chinese Communism: *Selected Documents*  TB/3031

BENJAMIN I. SCHWARTZ: Chinese Communism and the Rise of Mao  TB/1308

BENJAMIN I. SCHWARTZ: In Search of Wealth and Power: *Yen Fu and the West*  TB/1422

## Economics & Economic History

C. E. BLACK: The Dynamics of Modernization: *A Study in Comparative History*  TB/1321

STUART BRUCHEY: The Roots of American Economic Growth, 1607-1861: *An Essay in Social Causation. New Introduction by the Author.*  TB/1350

GILBERT BURCK & EDITORS OF *Fortune:* The Computer Age: *And its Potential for Management*  TB/1179

JOHN ELLIOTT CAIRNES: The Slave Power. ‡ *Edited with Introduction by Harold D. Woodman*  TB/1433

SHEPARD B. CLOUGH, THOMAS MOODIE & CAROL MOODIE, Eds.: Economic History of Europe: *Twentieth Century* #  HR/1388

THOMAS C.COCHRAN: The American Business System: *A Historical Perspective, 1900-1955*  TB/1180

ROBERT A. DAHL & CHARLES E. LINDBLOM: Politics, Economics, and Welfare: *Planning and Politico-Economic Systems Resolved into Basic Social Processes*  TB/3037

PETER F. DRUCKER: The New Society: *The Anatomy of Industrial Order*  TB/1082

HAROLD U. FAULKNER: The Decline of Laissez Faire, 1897-1917 ∧  TB/1397

PAUL W. GATES: The Farmer's Age: *Agriculture, 1815-1860* ∧  TB/1398

WILLIAM GREENLEAF, Ed.: American Economic Development Since 1860 +  HR/1353

J. L. & BARBARA HAMMOND: The Rise of Modern Industry. || *Introduction by R. M. Hartwell*  TB/1417

3

ROBERT L. HEILBRONER: The Future as History: *The Historic Currents of Our Time and the Direction in Which They Are Taking America* TB/1386

ROBERT L. HEILBRONER: The Great Ascent: *The Struggle for Economic Development in Our Time* TB/3030

FRANK H. KNIGHT: The Economic Organization TB/1214

DAVID S. LANDES: Bankers and Pashas: *International Finance and Economic Imperialism in Egypt. New Preface by the Author* TB/1412

ROBERT LATOUCHE: The Birth of Western Economy: *Economic Aspects of the Dark Ages* TB/1290

ABBA P. LERNER: Everbody's Business: *A Reexamination of Current Assumptions in Economics and Public Policy* TB/3051

W. ARTHUR LEWIS: Economic Survey, 1919-1939 TB/1446

W. ARTHUR LEWIS: The Principles of Economic Planning. *New Introduction by the Author°* TB/1436

ROBERT GREEN MC CLOSKEY: American Conservatism in the Age of Enterprise TB/1137

PAUL MANTOUX: The Industrial Revolution in the Eighteenth Century: *An Outline of the Beginnings of the Modern Factory System in England°* TB/1079

WILLIAM MILLER, Ed.: Men in Business: *Essays on the Historical Role of the Entrepreneur* TB/1081

GUNNAR MYRDAL: An International Economy. *New Introduction by the Author* TB/1445

HERBERT A. SIMON: The Shape of Automation: *For Men and Management* TB/1245

PERRIN STRYER: The Character of the Executive: *Eleven Studies in Managerial Qualities* TB/1041

RICHARD S. WECKSTEIN, Ed.: Expansion of World Trade and the Growth of National Economies ** TB/1373

Education

JACQUES BARZUN: The House of Intellect TB/1051
RICHARD M. JONES, Ed.: Contemporary Educational Psychology: *Selected Readings* ** TB/1292
CLARK KERR: The Uses of the University TB/1264

Historiography and History of Ideas

HERSCHEL BAKER: The Image of Man: *A Study of the Idea of Human Dignity in Classical Antiquity, the Middle Ages, and the Renaissance* TB/1047

J. BRONOWSKI & BRUCE MAZLISH: The Western Intellectual Tradition: *From Leonardo to Hegel* TB/3001

EDMUND BURKE: On Revolution. Ed. by Robert A. Smith TB/1401

WILHELM DILTHEY: Pattern and Meaning in History: *Thoughts on History and Society.° Edited with an Intro. by H. P. Rickman* TB/1075

ALEXANDER GRAY: The Socialist Tradition: *Moses to Lenin °* TB/1375

J. H. HEXTER: More's Utopia: *The Biography of an Idea. Epilogue by the Author* TB/1195

H. STUART HUGHES: History as Art and as Science: *Twin Vistas on the Past* TB/1207

ARTHUR O. LOVEJOY: The Great Chain of Being: *A Study of the History of an Idea* TB/1009

JOSE ORTEGA Y GASSET: The Modern Theme. *Introduction by Jose Ferrater Mora* TB/1038

RICHARD H. POPKIN: The History of Scepticism from Erasmus to Descartes. *Revised Edition* TB/1391

G. J. RENIER: History: *Its Purpose and Method* TB/1209

MASSIMO SALVADORI, Ed.: Modern Socialism # HR/1374

GEORG SIMMEL et al.: Essays on Sociology, Philosophy and Aesthetics. *Edited by Kurt H. Wolff* TB/1234

BRUNO SNELL: The Discovery of the Mind: *The Greek Origins of European Thought* TB/1018

W. WARREN WAGER, ed.: European Intellectual History Since Darwin and Marx TB/1297

W. H. WALSH: Philosophy of History: In Introduction TB/1020

History: General

HANS KOHN: The Age of Nationalism: *The First Era of Global History* TB/1380
BERNARD LEWIS: The Arabs in History TB/1029
BERNARD LEWIS: The Middle East and the West ° TB/1274

History: Ancient

A. ANDREWS: The Greek Tyrants TB/1103

ERNST LUDWIG EHRLICH: A Concise History of Israel: *From the Earliest Times to the Destruction of the Temple in A.D. 70 °* TB/128

ADOLF ERMAN, Ed.: The Ancient Egyptians: *A Sourcebook of their Writings. New Introduction by William Kelly Simpson* TB/1233

THEODOR H. GASTER: Thespis: *Ritual Myth and Drama in the Ancient Near East* TB/1281

MICHAEL GRANT: Ancient History ° TB/1190

A. H. M. JONES, Ed.: A History of Rome through the Fifgth Century # *Vol. I: The Republic* HR/1364
*Vol. II The Empire:* HR/1460

SAMUEL NOAH KRAMER: Sumerian Mythology TB/1055

NAPHTALI LEWIS & MEYER REINHOLD, Eds.: Roman Civilization *Vol. I: The Republic* TB/1231
*Vol. II: The Empire* TB/1232

History: Medieval

MARSHALL W. BALDWIN, Ed.: Christianity Through the 13th Century # HR/1468

MARC BLOCH: Land and Work in Medieval Europe. *Translated by J. E. Anderson* TB/1452

HELEN CAM: England Before Elizabeth TB/1026

NORMAN COHN: The Pursuit of the Millennium: *Revolutionary Messianism in Medieval and Reformation Europe* TB/1037

G. G. COULTON: Medieval Village, Manor, and Monastery HR/1022

HEINRICH FICHTENAU: The Carolingian Empire: *The Age of Charlemagne. Translated with an Introduction by Peter Munz* TB/1142

GALBERT OF BRUGES: The Murder of Charles the Good: *A Contemporary Record of Revolutionary Change in 12th Century Flanders. Translated with an Introduction by James Bruce Ross* TB/1311

F. L. GANSHOF: Feudalism TB/1058

F. L. GANSHOF: The Middle Ages: *A History of International Relations. Translated by Rémy Hall* TB/1411

W. O. HASSALL, Ed.: Medieval England: *As Viewed by Contemporaries* TB/1205

DENYS HAY: The Medieval Centuries ° TB/1192

DAVID HERLIHY, Ed.: Medieval Culture and Socitey # HR/1340

J. M. HUSSEY: The Byzantine World   TB/1057
ROBERT LATOUCHE: The Birth of Western Economy: *Economic Aspects of the Dark Ages* °   TB/1290
HENRY CHARLES LEA: The Inquisition of the Middle Ages. || *Introduction by Walter Ullmann*   TB/1456
FERDINAND LOT: The End of the Ancient World and the Beginnings of the Middle Ages. *Introduction by Glanville Downey*   TB/1044
H. R. LOYN: The Norman Conquest   TB/1457
ACHILLE LUCHAIRE: Social France at the time of Philip Augustus. *Intro. by John W. Baldwin*   TB/1314
GUIBERT DE NOGENT: Self and Society in Medieval France: *The Memoirs of Guibert de Nogent*. || Edited by John F. Benton   TB/1471
MARSILIUS OF PADUA: The Defender of Peace. *The Defensor Pacis. Translated with an Introduction by Alan Gewirth*   TB/1310
CHARLES PETIT-DUTAILLIS: The Feudal Monarchy in France and England: *From the Tenth to the Thirteenth Century* °   TB/1165
STEVEN RUNCIMAN: A History of the Crusades Vol. I: *The First Crusade and the Foundation of the Kingdom of Jerusalem. Illus.*   TB/1143
Vol. II: *The Kingdom of Jerusalem and the Frankish East 1100-1187. Illus.*   TB/1243
Vol. III: *The Kingdom of Acre and the Later Crusades. Illus.*   TB/1298
J. M. WALLACE-HADRILL: The Barbarian West: *The Early Middle Ages, A.D. 400-1000*   TB/1061

## History: Renaissance & Reformation

JACOB BURCKHARDT: The Civilization of the Renaissance in Italy. *Introduction by Benjamin Nelson and Charles Trinkaus. Illus.* Vol. I TB/40; Vol. II TB/41
JOHN CALVIN & JACOPO SADOLETO: A Reformation Debate. *Edited by John C. Olin*   TB/1239
FEDERICO CHABOD: Machiavelli and the Renaissance   TB/1193
THOMAS CROMWELL: Thomas Cromwell on Church and Commonwealth,: *Selected Letters 1523-1540.* ¶ *Ed. with an Intro. by Arthur J. Slavin*   TB/1462
R. TREVOR DAVIES: The Golden Century of Spain, 1501-1621 °   TB/1194
J. H. ELLIOTT: Europe Divided, 1559-1598 *a* °   TB/1414
G. R. ELTON: Reformation Europe, 1517-1559 ° *a*   TB/1270
DESIDERIUS ERASMUS: Christian Humanism and the Reformation: *Selected Writings. Edited and Translated by John C. Olin*   TB/1166
DESIDERIUS ERASMUS: Erasmus and His Age: *Selected Letters. Edited with an Introduction by Hans J. Hillerbrand. Translated by Marcus A. Haworth*   TB/1461
WALLACE K. FERGUSON et al.: Facets of the Renaissance. *Illus.*   TB/1098
WALLACE K. FERGUSON et al.: The Renaissance: *Six Essays. Illus.*   TB/1084
FRANCESCO GUICCIARDINI: History of Florence. *Translated with an Introduction and Notes by Mario Domandi*   TB/1470
WERNER L. GUNDERSHEIMER, Ed.: French Humanism, 1470-1600. * *Illus.*   TB/1473
MARIE BOAS HALL, Ed.: Nature and Nature's Laws: *Documents of the Scientific Revolution* #   HR/1420
HANS J. HILLERBRAND, Ed., The Protestant Reformation #   HR/1342
JOHAN HUIZINGA: Erasmus and the Age of Reformation. *Illus.*   TB/19

JOEL HURSTFIELD: The Elizabethan Nation   TB/1312
JOEL HURSTFIELD, Ed.: The Reformation Crisis   TB/1267
PAUL OSKAR KRISTELLER: Renaissance Thought: *The Classic, Scholastic, and Humanist Strains*   TB/1048
PAUL OSKAR KRISTELLER: Renaissance Thought II: *Papers on Humanism and the Arts*   TB/1163
PAUL O. KRISTELLER & PHILIP P. WIENER, Eds.: Renaissance Essays   TB/1392
DAVID LITTLE: Religion, Order and Law: *A Study in Pre-Revolutionary England.* § *Preface by R. Bellah*   TB/1418
NICCOLO MACHIAVELLI: History of Florence and of the Affairs of Italy: *From the Earliest Times to the Death of Lorenzo the Magnificent. Introduction by Felix Gilbert*   TB/1027
ALFRED VON MARTIN: Sociology of the Renaissance. ° *Introduction by W. K. Ferguson*   TB/1099
GARRETT MATTINGLY et al.: Renaissance Profiles. *Edited by J. H. Plumb*   TB/1162
J. E. NEALE: The Age of Catherine de Medici °   TB/1085
J. H. PARRY: The Establishment of the European Hegemony: 1415-1715: *Trade and Exploration in the Age of the Renaissance*   TB/1045
J. H. PARRY, Ed.: The European Reconnaissance: *Selected Documents* #   HR/1345
BUONACCORSO PITTI & GREGORIO DATI: Two Memoirs of Renaissance Florence: *The Diaries of Buonaccorso Pitti and Gregorio Dati. Edited with Intro. by Gene Brucker. Trans. by Julia Martines*   TB/1333
J. H. PLUMB: The Italian Renaissance: *A Concise Survey of Its History and Culture*   TB/1161
A. F. POLLARD: Henry VIII. *Introduction by A. G. Dickens.* °   TB/1249
RICHARD H. POPKIN: The History of Scepticism from Erasmus to Descartes   TB/139
PAOLO ROSSI: Philosophy, Technology, and the Arts, in the Early Modern Era 1400-1700. || *Edited by Benjamin Nelson. Translated by Salvator Attanasio*   TB/1458
FERDINAND SCHEVILL: The Medici. *Illus.* TB/1010
FERDINAND SCHEVILL: Medieval and Renaissance Florence. *Illus.* Vol. I: *Medieval Florence*   TB/1090
Vol. II: *The Coming of Humanism and the Age of the Medici*   TB/1091
R. H. TAWNEY: The Agrarian Problem in the Sixteenth Century. *Intro. by Lawrence Stone*   TB/1315
H. R. TREVOR-ROPER: The European Witch-craze of the Sixteenth and Seventeenth Centuries and Other Essays °   TB/1416
VESPASIANO: Rennaissance Princes, Popes, and *XVth Century: The Vespasiano Memoirs. Introduction by Myron P. Gilmore. Illus.*   TB/1111

## History: Modern European

RENE ALBRECHT-CARRIE, Ed.: The Concert of Europe #   HR/1341
MAX BELOFF: The Age of Absolutism, 1660-1815   TB/1062
OTTO VON BISMARCK: Reflections and Reminiscences. *Ed. with Intro. by Theodore S. Hamerow* ¶   TB/1357
EUGENE C. BLACK, Ed.: British Politics in the Nineteenth Century #   HR/1427

EUGENE C. BLACK, Ed.: European Political History, 1815-1870: *Aspects of Liberalism* ¶
TB/1331
ASA BRIGGS: The Making of Modern England, 1783-1867: *The Age of Improvement* °
TB/1203
D. W. BROGAN: The Development of Modern France ° Vol. I: *From the Fall of the Empire to the Dreyfus Affair* TB/1184
Vol. II: *The Shadow of War, World War I, Between the Two Wars* TB/1185
ALAN BULLOCK: Hitler, A Study in Tyranny. ° *Revised Edition. Illus.* TB/1123
EDMUND BURKE: On Revolution. *Ed. by Robert A. Smith* TB/1401
E. R. CARR: International Relations Between the Two World Wars. 1919-1939 ° TB/1279
E. H. CARR: The Twenty Years' Crisis, 1919-1939: *An Introduction to the Study of International Relations* ° TB/1122
GORDON A. CRAIG: From Bismarck to Adenauer: *Aspects of German Statecraft. Revised Edition* TB/1171
LESTER G. CROCKER, Ed.: The Age of Enlightenment # HR/1423
DENIS DIDEROT: The Encyclopedia: *Selections. Edited and Translated with Introduction by Stephen Gendzier* TB/1299
JACQUES DROZ: Europe between Revolutions, 1815-1848. ° *a Trans. by Robert Baldick* TB/1346
JOHANN GOTTLIEB FICHTE: Addresses to the German Nation. *Ed. with Intro. by George A. Kelly* ¶ TB/1366
FRANKLIN L. FORD: Robe and Sword: *The Re-Louis XIV* TB/1217
ROBERT & ELBORG FORSTER, Eds.: European Society in the Eighteenth Century # HR/1404
C. C. GILLISPIE: Genesis and Geology: *The Decades before Darwin* § TB/51
ALBERT GOODWIN, Ed.: The European Nobility in the Enghteenth Century TB/1313
ALBERT GOODWIN: The French Revolution TB/1064
ALBERT GUERARD: France in the Classical Age: *The Life and Death of an Ideal* TB/1183
JOHN B. HALSTED, Ed.: Romanticism # HR/1387
J. H. HEXTER: Reappraisals in History: *New Views on History and Society in Early Modern Europe* ° TB/1100
STANLEY HOFFMANN et al.: In Search of France: *The Economy, Society and Political System In the Twentieth Century* TB/1219
H. STUART HUGHES: The Obstructed Path: *French Social Thought in the Years of Desperation* TB/1451
JOHAN HUIZINGA: Dutch Civilisation in the 17th Century and Other Essays TB/1453
LIONAL KOCHAN: The Struggle for Germany: *1914-45* TB/1304
HANS KOHN: The Mind of Germany: *The Education of a Nation* TB/1204
HANS KOHN, Ed.: The Mind of Modern Russia: *Historical and Political Thought of Russia's Great Age* TB/1065
WALTER LAQUEUR & GEORGE L. MOSSE, Eds.: Education and Social Structure in the 20th Century. ° *Volume 6 of the Journal* of Contemporary History TB/1339
WALTER LAQUEUR & GEORGE L. MOSSE, Ed.: International Fascism, 1920-1945. ° *Volume 1 of the* Journal of Contemporary History TB/1276
WALTER LAQUEUR & GEORGE L. MOSSE, Eds.: Literature and Politics in the 20th Century. ° *Volume 5 of the* Journal of Contemporary History. TB/1328

WALTER LAQUEUR & GEORGE L. MOSSE, Eds.: The New History: *Trends in Historical Research and Writing Since World War II.* ° *Volume 4 of the* Journal of Contemporary History TB/1327
WALTER LAQUEUR & GEORGE L. MOSSE, Eds.: 1914: *The Coming of the First World War.* ° *Volume3 of the* Journal of Contemporary History TB/1306
C. A. MACARTNEY, Ed.: The Habsburg and Hohenzollern Dynasties in the Seventeenth and Eighteenth Centuries # HR/1400
JOHN MCMANNERS: European History, 1789-1914: *Men, Machines and Freedom* TB/1419
PAUL MANTOUX: The Industrial Revolution in the Eighteenth Century: *An Outline of the Beginnings of the Modern Factory System in England* TB/1079
FRANK E. MANUEL: The Prophets of Paris: *Turgot, Condorcet, Saint-Simon, Fourier, and Comte* TB/1218
KINGSLEY MARTIN: French Liberal Thought in the Eighteenth Century: *A Study of Political Ideas from Bayle to Condorcet* TB/1114
NAPOLEON III: Napoleonic Ideas: *Des Idées Napoléoniennes, par le Prince Napoléon-Louis Bonaparte. Ed. by Brison D. Gooch* ¶
TB/1336
FRANZ NEUMANN: Behemoth: *The Structure and Practice of National Socialism, 1933-1944* TB/1289
DAVID OGG: Europe of the Ancien Régime, 1715-1783 ° *a* TB/1271
GEORGE RUDE: Revolutionary Europe, 1783-1815 ° *a* TB/1272
MASSIMO SALVADORI, Ed.: Modern Socialism # TB/1374
HUGH SETON-WATSON: Eastern Europe Between the Wars, 1918-1941 TB/1330
DENIS MACK SMITH, Ed.: The Making of Italy, 1796-1870 # HR/1356
ALBERT SOREL: Europe Under the Old Regime. *Translated by Francis H. Herrick* TB/1121
ROLAND N. STROMBERG, Ed.: Realism, Naturalism, and Symbolism: *Modes of Thought and Expression in Europe, 1848-1914* # HR/1355
A. J. P. TAYLOR: From Napoleon to Lenin: *Historical Essays* ° TB/1268
A. J. P. TAYLOR: The Habsburg Monarchy, 1809-1918: *A History of the Austrian Empire and Austria-Hungary* ° TB/1187
J. M. THOMPSON: European History, 1494-1789 TB/1431
DAVID THOMSON, Ed.: France: Empire and Republic, 1850-1940 # HR/1387
ALEXIS DE TOCQUEVILLE & GUSTAVE DE BEAUMONT: Tocqueville and Beaumont on Social Reform. *Ed. and trans. with Intro. by Seymour Drescher* TB/1343
G. M. TREVELYAN: British History in the Nineteenth Century and After: *1792-1919* ° TB/1251
H. R. TREVOR-ROPER: Historical Essays ° TB/1269
W. WARREN WAGAR, Ed.: Science, Faith, and MAN: *European Thought Since 1914* # HR/1362
MACK WALKER, Ed.: Metternich's Europe, 1813-1848 # HR/1361
ELIZABETH WISKEMANN: Europe of the Dictators, 1919-1945 ° *a* TB/1273
JOHN B. WOLF: France: 1814-1919: *The Rise of a Liberal-Democratic Society* TB/3019

*Literature & Literary Criticism*

JACQUES BARZUN: The House of Intellect
TB/1051

6

BARRINGTON MOORE, JR.: Political Power and Social Theory: *Seven Studies* || TB/1221

BARRINGTON MOORE, JR.: Soviet Politics—The Dilemma of Power: *The Role of Ideas in Social Change* || TB/1222

BARRINGTON MOORE, JR.: Terror and Progress—USSR: *Some Sources of Change and Stability*

JOHN B. MORRALL: Political Thought in Medieval Times TB/1076

KARL R. POPPER: The Open Society and Its Enemies *Vol. I: The Spell of Plato* TB/1101
*Vol. II: The High Tide of Prophecy: Hegel, Marx, and the Aftermath* TB/1102

CONYERS READ, Ed.: The Constitution Reconsidered. *Revised Edition, Preface by Richard B. Morris* TB/1384

JOHN P. ROCHE, Ed.: Origins of American Political Thought: *Selected Readings* TB/1301

JOHN P. ROCHE, Ed.: American Political Thought: *From Jefferson to Progressivism* TB/1332

HENRI DE SAINT-SIMON: Social Organization, The Science of Man, and Other Writings. || *Edited and Translated with an Introduction by Felix Markham* TB/1152

CHARLES SCHOTTLAND, Ed.: The Welfare State ** TB/1323

JOSEPH A. SCHUMPETER: Capitalism, Socialism and Democracy TB/3008

PETER WOLL, Ed.: Public Administration and Policy: *Selected Essays* TB/1284

*Psychology*

ALFRED ADLER: The Individual Psychology of Alfred Adler: *A Systematic Presentation in Selections from His Writings. Edited by Heinz L. & Rowena R. Ansbacher* TB/1154

ALFRED ADLER: Problems of Neurosis: *A Book of Case Histories. Introduction by Heinz L. Ansbacher* TB/1145

LUDWIG BINSWANGER: Being-in-the-World: *Selected Papers.* || *Trans. with Intro. by Jacob Needleman* TB/1365

ARTHUR BURTON & ROBERT E. HARRIS: Clinical Studies of Personality Vol. I TB/3075
Vol. II TB/3076

HADLEY CANTRIL: The Invasion from Mars: *A Study in the Psychology of Panic* || TB/1282

MIRCEA ELIADE: Cosmos and History: *The Myth of the Eternal Return* § TB/2050

MIRCEA ELIADE: Myth and Reality TB/1369

MIRCEA ELIADE: Myths, Dreams and Mysteries: *The Encounter Between Contemporary Faiths and Archaic Realities* § TB/1320

MIRCEA ELIADE: Rites and Symbols of Initiation: *The Mysteries of Birth and Rebirth* § TB/1236

HERBERT FINGARETTE: The Self in Transformation: *Psychoanalysis, Philosophy and the Life of the Spirit* || TB/1177

SIGMUND FREUD: On Creativity and the Unconscious: *Papers on the Psychology of Art, Literature, Love, Religion.* § *Intro. by Benjamin Nelson* TB/45

J. GLENN GRAY: The Warriors: *Reflections on Men in Battle. Introduction by Hannah Arendt* TB/1294

WILLIAM JAMES: Psychology: *The Briefer Course. Edited with an Intro. by Gordon Allport* TB/1034

C. G. JUNG: Psychological Reflections. *Ed. by J. Jacobi* TB/2001

KARL MENNINGER, M.D.: Theory of Psychoanalytic Technique TB/1144

JOHN H. SCHAAR: Escape from Authority: *The Perspectives of Erich Fromm* TB/1155

MUZAFER SHERIF: The Psychology of Social Norms. *Introduction by Gardner Murphy* TB/3072

HELLMUT WILHELM: Change: *Eight Lectures on the I Ching* TB/2019

*Religion: Ancient and Classical, Biblical and Judaic Traditions*

W. F. ALBRIGHT: The Biblical Period from Abraham to Ezra TB/102

SALO W. BARON: Modern Nationalism and Religion TB/818

C. K. BARRETT, Ed.: The New Testament Background: *Selected Documents* TB/86

MARTIN BUBER: Eclipse of God: *Studies in the Relation Between Religion and Philosophy* TB/12

MARTIN BUBER: Hasidism and Modern Man. *Edited and Translated by Maurice Friedman* TB/839

MARTIN BUBER: The Knowledge of Man. *Edited with an Introduction by Maurice Friedman. Translated by Maurice Friedman and Ronald Gregor Smith* TB/135

MARTIN BUBER: Moses. *The Revelation and the Covenant* TB/837

MARTIN BUBER: The Origin and Meaning of Hasidism. *Edited and Translated by Maurice Friedman* TB/835

MARTIN BUBER: The Prophetic Faith TB/73

MARTIN BUBER: Two Types of Faith: *Interpenetration of Judaism and Christianity* ° TB/75

MALCOLM L. DIAMOND: Martin Buber: *Jewish Existentialist* TB/840

M. S. ENSLIN: Christian Beginnings TB/5

M. S. ENSLIN: The Literature of the Christian Movement TB/6

ERNST LUDWIG EHRLICH: A Concise History of Israel: *From the Earliest Times to the Destruction of the Temple in A.D. 70* ° TB/128

HENRI FRANKFORT: Ancient Egyptian Religion: *An Interpretation* TB/77

MAURICE S. FRIEDMAN: Martin Buber: *The Life of Dialogue* TB/64

ABRAHAM HESCHEL: The Earth Is the Lord's & The Sabbath. *Two Essays* TB/828

ABRAHAM HESCHEL: God in Search of Man: *A Philosophy of Judaism* TB/807

ABRAHAM HESCHEL: Man Is not Alone: *A Philosophy of Religion* TB/838

ABRAHAM HESCHEL: The Prophets: *An Introduction* TB/1421

T. J. MEEK: Hebrew Origins TB/69

JAMES MUILENBURG: The Way of Israel: *Biblical Faith and Ethics* TB/133

H. J. ROSE: Religion in Greece and Rome TB/55

H. H. ROWLEY: The Growth of the Old Testament TB/107

D. WINTON THOMAS, Ed.: Documents from Old Testament Times TB/85

*Religion: General Christianity*

ROLAND H. BAINTON: Christendom: *A Short History of Christianity and Its Impact on Western Civilization. Illus.*
Vol. I TB/131; Vol. II TB/132

JOHN T. MCNEILL: Modern Christian Movements. *Revised Edition* TB/1402

ERNST TROELTSCH: The Social Teaching of the Christian Churches. *Intro. by H. Richard Niebuhr* Vol. TB/71; Vol. II TB/72

## Religion: Early Christianity Through Reformation

ANSELM OF CANTERBURY: Truth, Freedom, and Evil: *Three Philosophical Dialogues. Edited and Translated by Jasper Hopkins and Herbert Richardson* TB/317

MARSHALL W. BALDWIN, Ed.: Christianity through the 13th Century # HR/1468

W. D. DAVIES: Paul and Rabbinic Judaism: *Some Rabbinic Elements in Pauline Theology. Revised Edition* ° TB/146

ADOLF DEISSMAN: Paul: *A Study in Social and Religious History* TB/15

JOHANNES ECKHART: Meister Eckhart: *A Modern Translation by R. Blakney* TB/8

EDGAR J. GOODSPEED: A Life of Jesus TB/1

ROBERT M. GRANT: Gnosticism and Early Christianity TB/136

WILLIAM HALLER: The Rise of Puritanism TB/22

GERHART B. LADNER: The Idea of Reform: *Its Impact on the Christian Thought and Action in the Age of the Fathers* TB/149

ARTHUR DARBY NOCK: Early Gentile Christianity and Its Hellenistic Background TB/111

ARTHUR DARBY NOCK: St. Paul ° TR/104

ORIGEN: On First Principles. *Edited by G. W. Butterworth. Introduction by Henri de Lubac* TB/311

GORDON RUPP: Luther's Progress to the Diet of Worms ° TB/120

## Religion: The Protestant Tradition

KARL BARTH: Church Dogmatics: *A Selection. Intro. by H. Gollwitzer. Ed. by G. W. Bromiley* TB/95

KARL BARTH: Dogmatics in Outline TB/56

KARL BARTH: The Word of God and the Word of Man TB/13

HERBERT BRAUN, et al.: God and Christ: *Existence and Province. Volume 5 of* Journal for Theology and the Church, *edited by Robert W. Funk and Gerhard Ebeling* TB/255

WHITNEY R. CROSS: The Burned-Over District: *The Social and Intellectual History of Enthusiastic Religion in Western New York, 1800-1850* TB/1242

NELS F. S. FERRE: Swedish Contributions to Modern Theology. *New Chapter by William A. Johnson* TB/147

WILLIAM R. HUTCHISON, Ed.: American Protestant Thought: *The Liberal Era* ‡ TB/1385

ERNST KASEMANN, et al.: Distinctive Protestant and Catholic Themes Reconsidered. *Volume 3 of* Journal for Theology and the Church, *edited by Robert W. Funk and Gerhard Ebeling* TB/253

SOREN KIERKEGAARD: On Authority and Revelation: *The Book on Adler, or a Cycle of Ethico-Religious Essays. Introduction by F. Sontag* TB/139

SOREN KIERKEGAARD: Crisis in the Life of an Actress, *and Other Essays on Drama. Translated with an Introduction by Stephen Crites* TB/145

SOREN KIERKEGAARD: Edifying Discourses. *Edited with an Intro. by Paul Holmer* TB/32

SOREN KIERKEGAARD: The Journals of Kierkegaard. ° *Edited with an Intro. by Alexander Dru* TB/52

SOREN KIERKEGAARD: The Point of View for My Work as an Author: *A Report to History.* § *Preface by Benjamin Nelson* TB/88

SOREN KIERKEGAARD: The Present Age. § *Translated and edited by Alexander Dru. Introduction by Walter Kaufmann* TB/94

SOREN KIERKEGAARD: Purity of Heart. *Trans. by Douglas Steere* TB/4

SOREN KIERKEGAARD: Repetition: *An Essay in Experimental Psychology* § TB/117

SOREN KIERKEGAARD: Works of Love: *Some Christian Reflections in the Form of Discourses* TB/122

WILLIAM G. MCLOUGHLIN, Ed.: The American Evangelicals: 1800-1900: *An Anthology* TB/1382

WOLFHART PANNENBERG, et al.: History and Hermeneutic. *Volume 4 of* Journal for Theology and the Church, *edited by Robert W. Funk and Gerhard Ebeling* TB/254

JAMES M. ROBINSON, et al.: The Bultmann School of Biblical Interpretation: New Directions? *Volume 1 of* Journal for Theology and the Church, *edited by Robert W. Funk and Gerhard Ebeling* TB/251

F. SCHLEIERMACHER: The Christian Faith. *Introduction by Richard R. Niebuhr.* Vol. I TB/108; Vol. II TB/109

F. SCHLEIERMACHER: On Religion: *Speeches to Its Cultured Despisers. Intro. by Rudolf Otto* TB/36

TIMOTHY L. SMITH: Revivalism and Social Reform: *American Protestantism on the Eve of the Civil War* TB/1229

PAUL TILLICH: Dynamics of Faith TB/42

PAUL TILLICH: Morality and Beyond TB/142

EVELYN UNDERHILL: Worship TB/10

## Religion: The Roman & Eastern Christian Traditions

A. ROBERT CAPONIGRI, Ed.: Modern Catholic Thinkers II: *The Church and the Political Order* TB/307

G. P. FEDOTOV: The Russian Religious Mind: *Kievan Christianity, the tenth to the thirteenth Centuries* TB/370

GABRIEL MARCEL: Being and Having: *An Existential Diary. Introduction by James Collins* TB/310

GABRIEL MARCEL: Homo Viator: *Introduction to a Metaphysic of Hope* TB/397

## Religion: Oriental Religions

TOR ANDRAE: Mohammed: *The Man and His Faith* § TB/62

EDWARD CONZE: Buddhism: *Its Essence and Development.* ° *Foreword by Arthur Waley* TB/58

EDWARD CONZE: Buddhist Meditation TB/1442

EDWARD CONZE et al, Editors: Buddhist Texts through the Ages TB/113

ANANDA COOMARASWAMY: Buddha and the Gospel of Buddhism TB/119

H. G. CREEL: Confucius and the Chinese Way TB/63

FRANKLIN EDGERTON, Trans. & Ed.: The Bhagavad Gita TB/115

SWAMI NIKHILANANDA, Trans. & Ed.: The Upanishads TB/114

D. T. SUZUKI: On Indian Mahayana Buddhism. ° *Ed. with Intro. by Edward Conze.* TB/1403

## Religion: Philosophy, Culture, and Society

NICOLAS BERDYAEV: The Destiny of Man TB/61

RUDOLF BULTMANN: History and Eschatology: *The Presence of Eternity* ° TB/91

RUDOLF BULTMANN AND FIVE CRITICS: Kerygma and Myth: *A Theological Debate* TB/80

RUDOLF BULTMANN and KARL KUNDSIN: Form Criticism: *Two Essays on New Testament Research. Trans. by F. C. Grant* TB/96
WILLIAM A. CLEBSCH & CHARLES R. JAEKLE: Pastoral Care in Historical Perspective: *An Essay with Exhibits* TB/148
FREDERICK FERRE: Language, Logic and God. *New Preface by the Author* TB/1407
LUDWIG FEUERBACH: The Essence of Christianity. § *Introduction by Karl Barth. Foreword by H. Richard Niebuhr* TB/11
C. C. GILLISPIE: Genesis and Geology: *The Decades before Darwin* § TB/51
ADOLF HARNACK: What Is Christianity? § *Introduction by Rudolf Bultmann* TB/17
KYLE HASELDEN: The Racial Problem in Christian Perspective TB/116
MARTIN HEIDEGGER: Discourse on Thinking. *Translated with a Preface by John M. Anderson and E. Hans Freund. Introduction by John M. Anderson* TB/1459
IMMANUEL KANT: Religion Within the Limits of Reason Alone. § *Introduction by Theodore M. Greene and John Silber* TB/FG
WALTER KAUFMANN, Ed.: Religion from Tolstoy to Camus: *Basic Writings on Religious Truth and Morals. Enlarged Edition* TB/123
JOHN MACQUARRIE: An Existentialist Theology: *A Comparison of Heidegger and Bultmann.* ° *Foreword by Rudolf Bultmann* TB/125
H. RICHARD NIERUHR: Christ and Culture TB/3
H. RICHARD NIEBUHR: The Kingdom of God in America TB/49
ANDERS NYGREN: Agape and Eros. *Translated by Philip S. Watson* ° TB/1430
JOHN H. RANDALL, JR.: The Meaning of Religion for Man. *Revised with New Intro. by the Author* TB/1379
WALTER RAUSCHENBUSCHS Christianity and the Social Crisis. ‡ *Edited by Robert D. Cross* TB/3059
JOACHIM WACH: Understanding and Believing. *Ed. with Intro. by Joseph M. Kitagawa* TB/1399

## Science and Mathematics

JOHN TYLER BONNER: The Ideas of Biology. Σ *Illus.* TB/570
W. E. LE GROS CLARK: The Antecedents of Man: *An Introduction to the Evolution of the Primates.* ° *Illus.* TB/559
ROBERT E. COKER: Streams, Lakes, Ponds. *Illus.* TB/586
ROBERT E. COKER: This Great and Wide Sea: *An Introduction to Oceanography and Marine Biology. Illus.* TB/551
W. H. DOWDESWELL: Animal Ecology. *61 illus.* TB/543
C. V. DURELL: Readable Relativity. *Foreword by Freeman J. Dyson* TB/530
GEORGE GAMOW: Biography of Physics. Σ *Illus.* TB/567
F. K. HARE: The Restless Atmosphere TB/560
S. KORNER: The Philosophy of Mathematics: *An Introduction* TB/547
J. R. PIERCE: Symbols, Signals and Noise: *The Nature and Process of Communication* Σ TB/574
WILLARD VAN ORMAN QUINE: Mathematical Logic TB/558

## Science: History

MARIE BOAS: The Scientific Renaissance, 1450-1630 ° TB/583
W. DAMPIER, Ed.: Readings in the Literature of Science. *Illus.* TB/512

STEPHEN TOULMIN & JUNE GOODFIELD: The Architecture of Matter: *The Physics, Chemistry and Physiology of Matter, Both Animate and Inanimate, as it has Evolved since the Beginnings of Science* TB/584
STEPHEN TOULMIN & JUNE GOODFIELD: The Discovery of Time TB/585
STEPHEN TOULMIN & JUNE GOODFIELD: The Fabric of the Heavens: *The Development of Astronomy and Dynamics* TB/579

## Science: Philosophy

J. M. BOCHENSKI: The Methods of Contemporary Thought. *Tr. by Peter Caws* TB/1377
J. BRONOWSKI: Science and Human Values. *Revised and Enlarged. Illus.* TB/505
WERNER HEISENBERG: Physics and Philosophy: *The Revolution in Modern Science. Introduction by F. S. C. Northrop* TB/549
KARL R. POPPER: Conjectures and Refutations: *The Growth of Scientific Knowledge* TB/1376
KARL R. POPPER: The Logic of Scientific Discovery TB/576
STEPHEN TOULMIN: Foresight and Understanding: *An Enquiry into the Aims of Science. Foreword by Jacques Barzun* TB/564
STEPHEN TOULMIN: The Philosophy of Science: *An Introduction* TB/513

## Sociology and Anthropology

REINHARD BENDIX: Work and Authority in Industry: *Ideologies of Management in the Course of Industrialization* TB/3035
BERNARD BERELSON, Ed., The Behavioral Sciences Today TB/1127
JOSEPH B. CASAGRANDE, Ed.: In the Company of Man: *Twenty Portraits of Anthropological Informants. Illus.* TB/3047
KENNETH B. CLARK: Dark Ghetto: *Dilemmas of Social Power. Foreword by Gunnar Myrdal* TB/1317
KENNETH CLARK & JEANNETTE HOPKINS: A Relevant War Against Poverty: *A Study of Community Action Programs and Observable Social Change* TB/1480
W. E. LE GROS CLARK: The Antecedents of Man: *An Introduction to the Evolution of the Primates.* ° *Illus.* TB/559
LEWIS COSER, Ed.: Political Sociology TB/1293
ROSE L. COSER, Ed.: Life Cycle and Achievement in America ** TB/1434
ALLISON DAVIS & JOHN DOLLARD: Children of Bondage: *The Personality Development of Negro Youth in the Urban South* ‖ TB/3049
ST. CLAIR DRAKE & HORACE R. CAYTON: Black Metropolis: *A Study of Negro Life in a Northern City. Introduction by Everett C. Hughes. Tables, maps, charts, and graphs* Vol. I TB/1086; Vol. II TB/1087
PETER F. DRUCKER: The New Society: *The Anatomy of Industrial Order* TB/1082
CORA DU BOIS: The People of Alor. *With a Preface by the Author* Vol. I *Illus.* TB/1042; Vol. II TB/1043
EMILE DURKHEIM et al.: Essays on Sociology and Philosophy: *with Appraisals of Durkheim's Life and Thought.* ‖ *Edited by Kurt H. Wolff* TB/1151
LEON FESTINGER, HENRY W. RIECKEN, STANLEY SCHACHTER: When Prophecy Fails: *A Social and Psychological Study of a Modern Group that Predicted the Destruction of the World* ‖ TB/1132

CHARLES Y. GLOCK & RODNEY STARK: Christian Beliefs and Anti-Semitism. *Introduction by the Authors* TB/1454

ALVIN W. GOULDNER: The Hellenic World TB/1479

ALVIN W. GOULDNER: Wildcat Strike: *A Study in Worker-Management Relationships* ‖ TB/1176

CESAR GRANA: Modernity and Its Discontents: *French Society and the French Man of Letters in the Nineteenth Century* TB/1318

L. S. B. LEAKEY: Adam's Ancestors: *The Evolution of Man and His Culture. Illus.* TB/1019

KURT LEWIN: Field Theory in Social Science: *Selected Theoretical Papers.* ‖ *Edited by Dorwin Cartwright* TB/1135

RITCHIE P. LOWRY: Who's Running This Town? *Community Leadership and Social Change* TB/1383

R. M. MACIVER: Social Causation TB/1153

GARY T. MARX: Protest and Prejudice: *A Study of Belief in the Black Community* TB/1435

ROBERT K. MERTON, LEONARD BROOM, LEONARD S. COTTRELL, JR., Editors: Sociology Today: *Problems and Prospects* ‖
Vol. I TB/1173; Vol. II TB/1174

GILBERT OSOFSKY, Ed.: The Burden of Race: A Documentary History of Negro-White Relations in America TB/1405

GILBERT OSOFSKY: Harlem: The Making of a Ghetto: *Negro New York 1890-1930* TB/1381

TALCOTT PARSONS & EDWARD A. SHILS, Editors: Toward a General Theory of Action: *Theoretical Foundations for the Social Sciences* TB/1083

PHILIP RIEFF: The Triumph of the Therapeutic: *Uses of Faith After Freud* TB/1360

JOHN H. ROHRER & MUNRO S. EDMONSON, Eds.: The Eighth Generation Grows Up: *Cultures and Personalities of New Orleans Negroes* ‖ TB/3050

ARNOLD ROSE: The Negro in America: *The Condensed Version of Gunnar Myrdal's* An American Dilemma. *Second Edition* TB/3048

GEORGE ROSEN: Madness in Society: *Chapters in the Historical Sociology of Mental Illness.* ‖ *Preface by Benjamin Nelson* TB/1337

PHILIP SELZNICK: TVA and the Grass Roots: *A Study in the Sociology of Formal Organization* TB/1230

PITIRIM A. SOROKIN: Contemporary Sociological Theories: *Through the First Quarter of the Twentieth Century* TB/3046

MAURICE R. STEIN: The Eclipse of Community: *An Interpretation of American Studies* TB/1128

WILLIAM I. THOMAS: The Unadjusted Girl: *With Cases and Standpoint for Behavior Analysis. Intro. by Michael Parenti* TB/1319

EDWARD A. TIRYAKIAN, Ed.: Sociological Theory, Values and Sociocultural Change: *Essays in Honor of Pitirim A. Sorokin* ° TB/1316

FERDINAND TONNIES: Community and Society: *Gemeinschaft und Gesellschaft. Translated and Edited by Charles P. Loomis* TB/1116

SAMUEL E. WALLACE: Skid Row as a Way of Life TB/1367

W. LLOYD WARNER and Associates: Democracy in Jonesville: *A Study in Quality and Inequality* ‖ TB/1129

W. LLOYD WARNER: Social Class in America: *The Evaluation of Status* TB/1013

FLORIAN ZNANIECKI: The Social Role of the Man of Knowledge. *Introduction by Lewis A. Coser* TB/1372